A SHORT
HISTORY OF
COFFEE

Pocket Essentials by Gordon Kerr

A SHORT HISTORY OF
COFFEE

GORDON KERR

Oldcastle Books

First published in 2021 by
Pocket Essentials, an imprint of
Oldcastle Books,
Harpenden, UK
www.oldcastlebooks.com
@oldcastlebooks

Editor: Nick Rennison

A CIP catalogue record for this book is available from the British Library.

ISBN
978-0-85730-420-9 (print)
978-0-85730-433-9 (ebook)

2 4 6 8 10 9 7 5 3 1

Typeset in 12.35 on 15pt Adobe Garamond Pro
by Avocet Typeset, Bideford, Devon, EX39 2BP
Printed and bound by CPI Group (UK) Ltd, Croydon, CR0 4YY

For Andy Baker and Jamie Ludbrook,
lovers of the bean.

CONTENTS

'Wherever it has been introduced it has spelled revolution. It has been the world's most radical drink in that its function has always been to make people think.'
William Ukers, *All About Coffee*, 1922

Introduction

Coffee – the world's favourite beverage. We drink around 2 billion cups of the stuff a day around the globe: at home; in down-at-heel cafés; in hipster coffee shops; in plush hotels and restaurants after meals; on trains and planes; and, hurriedly, without spilling it, on our way to meetings or work. It has become a modern phenomenon, our high streets lined by branches of the customary global and national brands as well as the one-offs, the independents, often run by coffee connoisseurs, catering for true coffee aficionados who are hungry for knowledge about the origins of the coffee bean that was picked, roasted, ground and brewed to give them a few minutes of pleasure or repose in a busy day.

Coffee started off as a rumour, part of a tale spun by travellers returning from the East, often merchants bringing back goods that were new and exciting – spices and silks, perhaps – who also spoke of this dark, reviving beverage that the people of those parts seemed to set such store by. The merchants remarked on how coffee invigorated them, how it kept them awake when sleep was inconveniently beckoning and how it was the conduit for good conversation and relaxation and escape from the cares of the long, hot day.

When it came to Europe and America, it was embraced and gave birth to the coffee shop. The coffee shop was about more than just drinking coffee and whatever else was on offer. It became a place where men – and it was men, because women were not welcome unless they were serving behind the counter – could transact business and, as the great seventeenth century diarist, Samuel Pepys, found in London, meet the right sort of people. There was no finer place for effective seventeenth century networking than Garraway's Coffee House or the Rainbow Coffee House in the City of London. Fortunes could be made and careers advanced over a cup of coffee, purchased for just a couple of pennies. Indeed, in both London and in the American colonies, coffee houses became serious places of business. Lloyd's of London developed in Edward Lloyd's Coffee House, the London Stock Exchange grew out of Jonathan's Coffee House, and in Merchants' coffee house, New York, the city's first financial institution, the Bank of New York, was created. Coffee houses were home to auctions, the sale of stocks and shares, and hubs of information about shipping and companies, as well as the latest gossip and intrigue about the royal court.

Momentous events were celebrated over cups of coffee in coffee houses but they were also created in them. In America, coffee houses were hotbeds of dissent in the eighteenth century, argument and discontent hanging in the smoky air. One of the most celebrated coffee-house taverns, the Green Dragon on Union Street in Boston became known as the 'headquarters of the Revolution', a meeting place for revolutionary generals itching to throw the British out of the 13 colonies, and Boston Tea Party conspirators planning their infamous action. Often the different loyalties of the clientele of coffee houses spilled over into outright violence. Debate over coffee stirred great emotions.

In France, too, the men behind the French Revolution aired their views over coffee and, indeed, the first act of the French Revolution, a stirring anti-government oration by the young journalist, Camille Desmoulins, took place outside Café Foy in Paris. In London, too, radicals and rebels intrigued and plotted in coffee houses to such an extent that Charles II almost closed them all down.

But coffee houses were also cultured places and still are. In Paris, the Impressionists would meet and complain in the café about their lack of sales and the disparagement of their art by critics. Writers, too, enjoyed the ambience of the coffee house and the bitter flavour of the dark drink.

Coffee also has a dark history, of course, and the slavery and exploitation that made fortunes for far too many can, and should, never be forgotten. The drink we have today is the result of a huge amount of suffering and loss of life. Wives were separated from husbands and children were ripped from the arms of their mothers in pursuit of the great wealth that coffee could bring. The fact that such exploitation still exists in parts of the world is reason enough for people to start questioning where their coffee comes from, as many who are eager participants in coffee's third wave do.

A Short History of Coffee investigates the legends and myths, the places, and the interesting and often eccentric characters who have helped to make coffee a staple of our daily lives. The book investigates coffee's origins in Ethiopia and Yemen and its spread through the Middle East before it was brought to Europe by intrepid travellers and merchants. As coffee became increasingly popular, coffee shops began to proliferate on the high streets and in the squares of towns and cities across Europe, creating new and exciting hubs of commerce, news and debate, where deals could be done and revolution could be incited. The book follows the development of this phenomenon and its growth in popularity through to the twenty first century explosion of coffee shop culture. It lifts the recyclable lid on the business as well as the pleasure of coffee. In the process, we learn that the story of our favourite drink is a frothy brew of business, politics, money and intrigue.

'A young goatherd named Kaldi noticed one day that his goats, whose deportment up to that time had been irreproachable, were abandoning themselves to the most extravagant prancings. The venerable buck, ordinarily so dignified and solemn, bounded about like a young kid. Kaldi attributed this foolish gaiety to certain fruits of which the goats had been eating with delight. The story goes that the poor fellow had a heavy heart; and in the hope of cheering himself up a little, he thought he would pick and eat of the fruit. The experiment succeeded marvelously. He forgot his troubles and became the happiest herder in happy Arabia. When the goats danced, he gaily made himself one of the party, and entered into their fun with admirable spirit. One day, a monk chanced to pass by and stopped in surprise to find a ball going on. A score of goats were executing lively pirouettes like a ladies' chain, while the buck solemnly balancé-ed , and the herder went through the figures of an eccentric pastoral dance. The astonished monk inquired the cause of this saltatorial madness; and Kaldi told him of his precious discovery. Now, this poor monk had a great sorrow; he always went to sleep in the middle of his prayers; and he reasoned that Mohammed without doubt was revealing this marvelous fruit to him to overcome his sleepiness.'

French version of the legend of *Kaldi*

'Coffee joins men, born for society, in a more perfect union; protestations are more sincere in being made at a time when the mind is not clouded with fumes and vapors, and therefore not easily forgotten, which too frequently happens when made over a bottle.'

Antoine Galland (1646-1715), French archaeologist and translator of *The Arabian Nights*

1

Origins

Ethiopia and a Boy and His Goats

The coffee plant has its origins in Abyssinia and Arabia, initially growing wild there, but its cultivation spread throughout the tropics. But at what point in distant history did it start its journey towards being a vital part of our daily routine? And how did it begin that journey? Was it a food to begin with or, perhaps, an infusion? Maybe it started out as a brew, or a medicine. Perhaps it was all of these at the same time.

That may all be lost in the mists of time, but what we do know is that coffee came from the area in which the bones of the earliest hominids have been discovered, although it cannot be confirmed that its lineage stretches back to that time around four-and-a-half million years ago when *Ardipithecus ramidus* was walking the earth. The birthplace of *Coffea arabica* – the coffee shrub – was, as with the earliest hominid, in the isolated and beautiful Harenna

Forest in the imposing Bale Mountains which rise up about 100 kilometres to the southeast of the capital of modern-day Ethiopia. The baboons of the area still enjoy coffee berries and the uplifting effect that they have on their state of mind.

The drink with which we are so familiar did not develop immediately and, in fact, it was probably many thousands of years before it appeared. Coffee berries were probably used for medicinal purposes to begin with, giving energy to the nomadic peoples of Ethiopia and Arabia who would often have to endure long and arduous journeys in their search for new pastures for their sheep and goats. The restorative powers of coffee berries were more likely to have been discovered by those who had an interest in plants and herbs. Thus, healers, shamans and herbalists experimented and discovered which particular qualities could be derived from individual plants and herbs. There is evidence that the coffee berry was pounded into a pulp, sometimes after being roasted, but not always. It was then mixed with fat to be used as an energising spread that was eaten on bread of some kind. The coffee berry was used in this manner for thousands of years in the highlands of Ethiopia. But, leaves and berries were also brewed with hot water to make a weak tea. The sweet beverage *qisr* – now known as *kisher* – was made using the husks of the coffee berry, lightly roasted. The pulp was even sometimes fermented to make a kind of wine.

However, it was still some way from the invigorating drink that we know and love today.

The Rapid Spread of Coffee

The first mention of coffee in print appears in the writings of the Persian polymath and physician, Abū Bakr Muhammad ibn Zakariyya al-Razi (854-925 AD), known to the West as Rhazes. In his writings, he mentions a drink called *bunchum*, describing it as 'hot and dry and very good for the stomach'. Around 1000 AD, another Arab physician, Abu Ali Sina (980-1037), known in the West as Avicenna, also wrote about *bunchum*:

> As to the choice thereof, that of a lemon color, light, and of a good smell, is the best; the white and the heavy is naught. It is hot and dry in the first degree, and, according to others, cold in the first degree. It fortifies the members, it cleans the skin, and dries up the humidities that are under it, and gives an excellent smell to all the body.

Of course, the beverage about which these two men were writing was far from the coffee with which we are familiar. Nonetheless, its spread from Ethiopia was rapid, as it was carried across the Red Sea by Arab traders. Soon, the Arabs were enjoying the pleasures of coffee. There is even a legend that says that the Prophet Muhammad claimed that after drinking coffee he could 'unhorse forty men and possess forty women'.

The Ethiopians established coffee plantations in Yemen when they conquered and ruled that country for 50 years in the sixth century and they called the drink that was produced *qahwa*. This is the Arabic word for 'a brew' and the English word coffee is derived from it. In fact, the word 'coffee' entered the English language in 1582, taken from the Dutch *koffie*. This, in turn, comes from the Ottoman Turkish *kahve* which is itself derived from *qahwa*. *Qahwa* may, in fact, be a reference to the use of coffee as an appetite suppressant, the Arabic word *qahiya* meaning 'to lack hunger'. The Arabic root, *qhh*, means 'dark colour' and *qahwah*, the feminine form of *qahwa*, also meant 'wine', a drink dark in colour.

The first reliable date for a written reference to coffee is 1454. The mufti of Aden, Muhammad Ibn Said Al Dhabhani, was an importer of goods from Ethiopia to Yemen, and first became acquainted with the drink on a journey through Abyssinia. When he returned home to Aden, he fell ill. He remembered the dark bitter beverage he had seen being drunk in Abyssinia and wondered whether it might improve his health. He asked for some to be sent to him and it did, indeed, lead to an improvement in his wellbeing. But not only did it improve his health, he also realised that it helped to stave off sleep. Therefore, he gave his approval to its use by the religious personages known as the dervishes, believing that it would give them the energy to 'spend the night in prayers or other religious exercises with more attention and presence of mind'.

This recommendation by a revered figure such as the mufti, who was well-known for his knowledge of science and religious matters, turned coffee into a hugely fashionable drink in Yemen and from there it spread to other countries. It was adopted by lawyers, students and those who worked or travelled at night and required something to keep them going through the dark hours. Coffee overtook another popular drink, *khat* or *cat*, which was brewed using the leaves of a plant of the same name.

By the end of the fifteenth century, the cultivation of coffee had spread from Yemen to Mecca and Medina where it was used, as in the case of the dervishes, for religious purposes. By 1510, the dervishes in Cairo were drinking it to stay awake. It was served in a large red earthenware jar and the head dervish dispensed it to his monks in a small bowl which he filled from the jar. While drinking, they recited their prayers. When it had made its circuit of the dervishes, it was passed to the members of the congregation. Thus, coffee assumed a religious role, every religious ceremony or festival featuring the drinking of the beverage. But it also moved beyond the bounds of religious ritual. The people of Mecca began drinking it purely for pleasure in *kahve kanes*, the earliest coffee houses. They drank it while they played chess and other games, debated the politics of the day or danced and sang and played music. Some saw this behaviour as scandalous. Devout Muslims, especially, found the behaviour in coffee houses outrageous. Nonetheless, it spread through the Islamic world, to Persia, Turkey, Egypt and across North Africa.

As it grew in popularity throughout the sixteenth century, however, it began to make enemies who were disdainful of the enjoyment people were deriving from frequenting coffee houses, where, according to reports, there was gambling and even sexual shenanigans. But, coffee houses were also places where people could express their feelings about those in power. One night in 1511, as he was leaving the mosque, the governor of Mecca, a strict disciplinarian named Hayir Bey (died 1522), saw a group of men drinking in a corner. They were making preparations for a night of prayer. He thought, at first, that they must be drinking wine, but was told that it was actually coffee. Informed that everyone in the city drank coffee, he carried out an investigation and concluded that this drink needed to be suppressed. He called his religious, medical and legal advisers to a meeting and explained what he had seen at the mosque. He explained about coffee houses, that many indulgences took place in them. Musical instruments were played, people danced and games were played for money, all contrary to the holy law. Some of the assembled dignitaries defended the beverage but eventually the other side held sway and an edict was drawn up banning coffee. It was dispatched to the sultan in Cairo. It stated that the coffee houses of Mecca were to be closed forthwith and the sale and drinking of coffee, either in public or private, was forbidden. Coffee stored in warehouses in the city was burned. Of course, the edict was hugely unpopular given that, by this time, many people could not do without their coffee fix. There was outspoken opposition to the ban and many were outraged by what they saw as an ill-informed and unfair decision. The ban was breached by many in private. It was pointed out that the mufti, a personage whose opinion usually carried a great deal of weight in an Arab community, had spoken in favour of the beverage. Nonetheless, punishments for breaches were carried out, and one man was led through the streets of the city astride an ass after he had been severely beaten.

All did not go well with the edict, however. The Ottoman Turkish Sultan Suleiman I (r. 1520-1566) expressed his disapproval of what he saw as the 'indiscreet zeal' of the governor of Mecca and his advisers, and persuaded Grand Mufti Mehmet Ebussuud el-imadi (1490-1574) to issue a *fatwa* rescinding the ban on coffee and coffee shops. The governor of Mecca was reprimanded by the sultan for his action in banning something which was perfectly acceptable in Cairo and the prohibition was immediately lifted. Those who enjoyed coffee might have seen some justice in the eventual fate of the governor who was convicted of being an extortionist and thief and tortured to death.

The sixteenth century saw further bans on coffee. In Mecca, again, in 1524, the *kadi* – a type of judge who presides over matters of Islamic law – closed down all the coffee houses, but on this occasion his ban did not extend to drinking at home in private. No sooner had his successor as *kadi* been appointed than they were all opened up again.

Coffee in Ottoman Turkey

Coffee arrived in Constantinople in 1517, introduced by Sultan Selim I (r. 1512-1520) after he had conquered Egypt. Some 13 years later, it had arrived in Damascus, capital of Syria, and the inhabitants of Aleppo were drinking it by around 1532. In 1534, opposition to the consumption of coffee once again manifested itself when a preacher in a Cairo mosque announced to listeners that those who drank coffee were not true followers of Muhammad. This immediately caused a riot, worshippers attacking a coffee house and burning it to the ground. Cairo was now split into two opposing camps – those who saw no harm in drinking coffee and those who insisted that its consumption was contrary to Islamic law. The city's chief justice searched for a solution, summoning medical advisers who told him that this matter had been examined previously and that the verdict had been in coffee's favour. They advised him that he should put a stop to the zeal of the bigots and unsubstantiated pronouncements by preachers. He complied, and ordered coffee to be served to everyone at the meeting, thus calming the situation.

In Constantinople, capital of the Ottoman Empire, there were also problems when coffee was first introduced. It was greeted with political intrigue, religious disapproval and unnecessary interference by civil authorities. None of this inhibited the drink's progress there, however, and Constantinople's coffee houses attained legendary status. Even though the drink had been consumed in the city since 1517, its first coffee houses did not open until 1554. The first proprietors were two Syrians – one named Schemsi who was from Damascus and another named Hekem, who was from Aleppo. Their establishments were both located in the Taktacalah quarter, and were similar in décor, with sofas and couches for customers to laze on. Soon there were numerous coffee houses in Constantinople and coffee became popular with all classes. The sultan even had officials – *kahvedjibachi* – to prepare and serve his coffee. As they became increasingly popular places to spend time in, the *kahve kanes*, as they were called, became even more sumptuous in both décor and furnishings. Lush carpets and various lavish entertainments awaited the coffee aficionado. Business was also transacted within their walls. Coffee houses welcomed lawyers, court officials, officials from the provinces on visits to the capital, teachers and professors. Merchants and travellers from all corners of the known world came to enjoy the delights of the *kahve kane*.

Their popularity led once more to persecution, however. Around 1570, Muslim religious leaders started to protest about coffee, principally because the coffee houses were full while their mosques were empty. Some went as far as to insist that it was more sinful to go to a coffee house than to a tavern selling alcohol. They claimed – perhaps wrongly, if the earlier story is to be believed – that Muhammad had not known coffee and it must, therefore, be a sin for his followers to drink it. The mufti, already an opponent of the beverage, found a useful loophole that gave him cause to close down the coffee houses. He pointed out that coffee was burned and ground to a charcoal-like substance before it was made into a drink and charcoal was, according to the Koran, an unsanitary foodstuff. As had happened elsewhere, however, people would not be denied their favourite beverage and coffee continued to be consumed in private. Even in 1580, after Murad III (r. 1574-95) declared coffee should be classed with wine and prohibited in accordance with the law of the

Prophet, people persisted with their illicit consumption. In fact, many coffee 'speakeasies' opened, in the backs of shops and other secret places where people gathered to drink and debate the weighty matters of the day, or just relax and enjoy themselves. Eventually, a mufti came along who reinstated coffee-drinking.

During the reign of Murad IV (r. 1623-40) coffee lovers once again had their enjoyment curtailed. Fearing unrest during a contentious war with Candia (present-day Crete), the Grand Vizier Köprülü Mehmed Pasha (1583-1661) again ordered the coffee houses to be closed. He believed them to be breeding grounds for sedition and gathering places for opponents of the government. The vizier was something of a dictator and ruthlessly enforced his ban, with severe punishment for breaching it. A first offence resulted in a serious beating. A second breach resulted in the offender being sewn into a leather bag and thrown into the Bosporus to drown. Even with such harsh penalties, however, people would not be stopped, and they persisted with their clandestine coffee consumption. They carried on partly because caffeine is, of course, in the minds of some experts, at least, addictive, although unlike many other addictions, it does not come with ill effects. It is also a stimulant, of both the body and the intellect. But, importantly, it is also a social enabler and the environments in which it was drunk back then – coffee houses – provided opportunities for business to be conducted, poetry to be recited and written, as well as for entertainment and debate. Interestingly, the vizier did not close the city's taverns, perhaps not quite concurring with what Antoine Galland (1646-1715), French archaeologist and translator of *The Arabian Nights* said:

> Coffee joins men, born for society, in a more perfect union; protestations are more sincere in being made at a time when the mind is not clouded with fumes and vapors, and therefore not easily forgotten, which too frequently happens when made over a bottle.

When the crisis was over, and he no longer saw the coffee houses as a threat to his government, the vizier relented and, to the great joy of the inhabitants of the city, allowed them to re-open. Thereafter, coffee became so important to life and culture in Turkey that the lack of sufficient supplies of it in a household provided sufficient grounds for a woman to divorce her husband.

Middle-Eastern Coffee Houses

Some sources have claimed that Persia was the first place to discover coffee as a drink, but it seems a somewhat spurious claim. Nonetheless, as in Ethiopia, coffee has been around there for a very long time, as have coffee houses. Instead of viewing them with suspicion as the ruling elite in Turkey did, however, the Persian ruling faction sought to embrace them. In fact, the wife of ruler, Shah Abbas I (r.1571-1629), was so impressed by the way people gathered in the main coffee house of Isfahan to debate politics and other weighty matters, that she installed a leading religious official there permanently to enlighten coffee drinkers on the finer points of religion, law and history. It was a smart move as it steered all conversation away from the political controversies of the day. Other coffee houses did the same and this enabled the state to control them, preventing them from becoming hotbeds of sedition and unrest.

One German traveller provided a description of these early Middle-Eastern coffee houses:

> They are commonly large halls, having their floors spread with mats, and illuminated at night by a multitude of lamps. Being the only theatres for the exercise of profane eloquence, poor scholars attend here to amuse the people. Select portions are read, e.g. the adventures of Rustan Sal, a Persian hero. Some aspire to the praise of invention, and compose tales and fables. They walk up and down as they recite, or assuming oratorial consequence, harangue upon subjects chosen by themselves.
>
> In one coffee house at Damascus an orator was regularly hired to tell his stories at a fixed hour; in other cases, he was more directly dependent upon the taste of his hearers, as at the conclusion of his discourse, whether it had consisted of literary topics or of loose and idle tales, he looked to the audience for a voluntary contribution.

In other coffee houses, there might be dancers and people reciting the fantastic tales of *The Arabian Nights*.

For centuries, the beverage retained religious connotations, even as it became more secularised and people increasingly drank it purely for pleasure and leisure. It was drunk at least several times a day in houses, no matter the class or financial status of the household and some people are even said to have drunk as many as 20 dishes of coffee a day. Always offered to visitors, it became part of the social rituals of everyday existence. In fact, to refuse a cup of coffee came to be regarded as a great insult.

The Turks continued to take their consumption of the beverage to extremes. In the larger houses of the wealthy ruling elite there were servants whose sole responsibility was making coffee. The servant in charge of such employees was the *Kavveghi* – the Steward of the Coffee. In a harem, or a seraglio, there would be a number of such men and they could have as many as 50 others under them. The coffee was served on salvers of silver or painted or varnished wood, holding 15 to 20 silver dishes of coffee, by *Itchoglans* – special coffee pages.

The Swedish traveller and envoy to the Ottoman Empire, Nicholas Rolamb, in his *Relation of a Journey to Constantinople in 1657*, describes the important role coffee played in Turkish domestic life:

This [coffee] is a kind of pea that grows in Egypt, which the Turks pound and boil in water, and take it for pleasure instead of brandy, sipping it through the lips boiling hot, persuading themselves that it consumes catarrhs, and prevents the rising of vapours out of the stomach into the head. The drinking of this coffee and smoking tobacco (for tho' the use of tobacco is forbidden on pain of death, yet it is used in Constantinople more than anywhere by men as well as women, tho' secretly) makes up all the pastime among the Turks, and is the only thing they treat one another with; for which reason all people of distinction have a particular room next their own, built on purpose for it, where there stands a jar of coffee continually boiling.

Early European Encounters with Coffee

In 1582, the German physician and botanist, Leonhard Rauwolf (1535-96), was the first European to mention coffee. Rauwolf's travels are described in Chapter 2 of this book.

Edward Pococke (1604-91) was an English Orientalist, Church of England priest and biblical scholar who sailed for Aleppo in 1630 as chaplain to an English merchant. There, he studied Arabic and collected many significant manuscripts. He furthered his studies and collected more books and manuscripts in Constantinople several years later. He will have encountered coffee in these places but also found references to it in the writings he brought back to England. Coffee is described rather alarmingly, for example, in his 1659 translation, *The Nature of the Drink Kauhi, or Coffee, and the Berry of which it is Made, Described by an Arabian Phisitian*:

Bun is a plant in Yaman [Yemen], which is planted in Adar, and groweth up and is gathered in Ab. It is about a cubit high, on a stalk about the thickness of one's thumb. It flowers white, leaving a berry like a small nut, but that sometimes it is broad like a bean; and when it is peeled, parteth in two. The best of it is that which is weighty and yellow; the worst, that which is black. It is hot in the first degree, dry in the second: it is usually reported to be cold and dry, but it is not so; for it is bitter, and whatsoever is bitter is hot. It may be that the scorce is hot, and the Bun it selfe either of equall temperature, or cold in the first degree.

That which makes for its coldnesse is its stipticknesse. In summer it is by experience found to conduce to the drying of rheumes, and flegmatick coughes and distillations, and the opening of obstructions, and the provocation of urin. It is now known by the name of Kohwah. When it is dried and thoroughly boyled, it allayes the ebullition of the blood, is good against the small poxe and measles, the bloudy pimples; yet causeth vertiginous headheach, and maketh lean much, occasioneth waking, and the Emrods, and asswageth lust, and sometimes breeds melancholly.

He that would drink it for livelinesse sake, and to discusse slothfulnesse, and the other properties that we have mentioned, let him use much sweat meates with it, and oyle of pistaccioes, and butter. Some drink it with milk, but it is an error, and such as may bring in danger of the leprosy.

Coffee does not appear in Ancient Greek or Roman writings although the Italian composer and author, Pietro della Valle (1586-1652), reckoned that when Homer wrote about the *nepenthe* that Helen took with her out of Egypt to assuage her sorrow, he was actually referring to coffee mixed with wine. This claim is disputed, however. A number of British authors have suggested that the 'black broth' of the Lacedaemonians (Spartans) was, in fact, coffee. The German theologian Georg Pasch (1661-1707) wrote in his 1700 Latin treatise, *New Discoveries Made since the Time of the Ancients*, that in the Bible, 1 Samuel, xxv, 18, the five measures of parched corn that were amongst the presents that King David was given by his wife Abigail in order to assuage his anger were actually coffee.

The Swiss-French Protestant minister and political writer Pierre Étienne Louis Dumont (1759-1829) claimed that it was coffee and not lentils that was the 'red pottage' for which Esau sold his birthright. He also proposed that the parched grain Boaz ordered to be given to Ruth in the Old Testament was roasted coffee berries.

Legends and Myths

Several Islamic legends claim that Muslims were the first to use coffee as a beverage. One tells how, around 1258, a certain Omar, a disciple of the legendary founder of the Yemeni town of Mocha, Sheik Abul Hasan ash-Shadhili (1196-1258), stumbled upon coffee at Ousab (now Wusab) in Arabia, after he was sent into exile there as punishment for his moral failings. The Sheik and his followers were starving but they gorged upon the berries of nearby coffee plants. The berries were bitter, so in order to make them taste better, they boiled them in water and they were revived by the drink. In Ousab, Omar who was a physician and a priest, treated patients successfully with this beverage. Stories of the curative powers of the drink produced from the berries reached Mocha and led to an invitation to return to the city in triumph. The governor even built him and his followers a monastery. There are, in fact, many versions of this legend. One relates that:

The dervish Hadji Omar was driven by his enemies out of Mocha into the desert, where they expected he would die of starvation. This undoubtedly would have occurred if he had not plucked up courage to taste some strange berries which he found growing on a shrub. While they seemed to be edible, they were very bitter; and he tried to improve the taste by roasting them. He found, however, that they had become very hard, so he attempted to soften them with water. The berries seemed to remain as hard as before, but the liquid turned brown, and Omar drank it on the chance that it contained some of the nourishment from the berries. He was amazed at how it refreshed him, enlivened his sluggishness, and raised his drooping spirits. Later, when he returned to Mocha, his salvation was considered a miracle. The beverage to which it was due sprang into high favour, and Omar himself was made a saint.

One of the most famous of the legends surrounding the origin of coffee features a young goatherd named Kaldi. The tale of Kaldi has been told not just in Ethiopia but also in Egypt, Turkey, Syria, Iraq, Iran and Yemen. The tale varies slightly from country to country but it basically recounts how a young goatherd, Kaldi, complained to the abbot of a nearby monastery that the goats he was looking after became very frisky after nibbling on the berries of shrubs close to their pastures. Curious, the abbot decided to try some of the berries himself. He also found himself energised by them and, as a result, ordered that some be boiled and that the resulting beverage be drunk by his monks who had been finding it difficult to stay awake during services in the middle of the night. To his delight, he discovered that the drink helped them to get through their midnight rituals. News of the restorative powers of these miraculous berries rapidly spread and soon everyone wanted them.

There is also a legend that Muhammad was given the secret of coffee by the angel Gabriel, as suggested by a passage in the Koran: 'They shall be given to drink an excellent wine; its seal is that of the musk'. It is unlikely, however, that coffee was known at that time, or that the ancients or those living in biblical times knew of it. Rhazes was working 200 years after Muhammad's death and there is no evidence of coffee before his time. Tea, on the other hand, has a longer provenance, pre-dating the Christian era.

In 793, for instance, during the Tang dynasty in China, tea was cultivated and taxes are recorded as being levied on it. It was certainly known to Arab traders during the following century.

'Paris became one vast café. Conversation in France was at its zenith. There were less eloquence and rhetoric than in '89. With the exception of Rousseau, there was no orator to cite. The intangible flow of wit was as spontaneous as possible. For this sparkling outburst there is no doubt that honour should be ascribed in part to the auspicious revolution of the times, to the great event which created new customs, and even modified human temperament – the advent of coffee.'

Jules Michelet (1798-1874), French historian

2

Coffee Comes to Western Europe

Leonhard Rauwolf

In 1573, German physicist, botanist and traveller, Leonhard Rauwolf (1535-1596), set off on a trip to the Near East, the first European botanist after medieval times to visit Syria and Mesopotamia. His trip was financed by his brother-in-law who hoped that he would return with new plants and drugs that could be profitable for his company.

Rauwolf travelled from his home in Augsburg to Marseilles from where he set sail for Tripoli in Lebanon. He journeyed on to Aleppo, remaining there for a couple of months. In 1574, he travelled to Baghdad and Mosul in modern-day Iraq, which was at the time under the control of the Ottoman Turks. The following year took Rauwolf to Jerusalem and, in 1576, he finally returned home to Augsburg. Shortly after he got back, he published his botanical observations in *Viertes Kreutterbuch darein vil schoene und fremde Kreutter* (*Fourth Book of Herbs in Which are Many Beautiful and Strange Herbs*). He also published observations of the countries and cultures through which he passed, in *Aigentliche Beschreibung der Raiß inn die Morgenländerin* (published in English in 1693 as *Dr Leonhart Rauwolf's Travels into the Eastern Countries*). Rauwolf was one of the first Europeans to describe the drinking of coffee, at that time completely unknown in Europe, and he was the first to refer to it in print:

If you have a mind to eat something or to drink other liquors, there is commonly an open shop near it, where you sit down upon the ground or carpets and drink together. Among the rest they have a very good drink, by them called *Chaube* [coffee] that is almost as black as ink, and very good in illness, chiefly that of the stomach; of this they drink in the morning early in open places before everybody, without any fear or regard, out of China cups, as hot as they can; they put it often to their lips but drink but little at a time, and let it go round as they sit. In this same water they take a fruit called *Bunnu* which in its bigness, shape and colour is almost like unto a bayberry, with two thin shells surrounded, which, as they informed me, are brought from the Indies; but as these in themselves are, and have within them, two yellowish grains in two distinct cells, and besides, being they agree in their virtue, figure, looks, and name with the *Bunchum* of Avicenna, and *Bunca*, of Rasis ad Almans [Rhazes] exactly; therefore I take them to be the same, until I am better informed by the learned. This liquor is very common among them, wherefore there are a great many of them that sell it, and others that sell the berries, everywhere in their *Batzars*.

In 1588, the decidedly Protestant Rauwolf left his home town of Augsburg when the town's leaders reverted to Catholicism. After serving as a physician in the town of Linz for eight years, he joined the imperial troops fighting the Turks in Hungary. He died at Waitzen, now Vac in Hungary, that same year.

Coffee Arrives in Italy

No one can say for sure exactly when coffee came to Europe from Constantinople, but it seems possible that it would have been the Venetians who initially brought it back with them from the Levant, an area with which they carried out a great deal of trade. The *Signoria* – Venice's governing authority – provided accommodation for a number of Turkish merchants in the Rialto area of the city and it is almost certain that they would have drunk coffee while there. This is confirmed, in fact, in an inventory of the belongings of a Turkish merchant, Huseyin Çelebi, who was murdered in Venice in 1575. Amongst the items is a *finjan*, a vessel used in coffee-making.

It was in Venice that the first description of the coffee plant was printed, in *The Plants of Egypt*, by Paduan physician and botanist, Prospero Alpini (1553-1617). Written in Latin, it was published in 1592. Alpini describes first seeing the coffee tree:

> I have seen this tree at Cairo, it being the same tree that produces the fruit, so common in Egypt, to which they give the name *bon* or *ban*. The Arabians and the Egyptians make a sort of decoction of it, which they drink instead of wine; and it is sold in all their public houses, as wine is with us. They call this drink *caova*. The fruit of which they make it comes from 'Arabia the Happy' [*Arabia Felix*] and the tree that I saw looks like a spindle tree, but the leaves are thicker, tougher, and greener. The tree is never without leaves.

The German botanist Johann Vesling (1598-1649) worked at the medical college in Venice. In 1628, he travelled to Egypt and Jerusalem where he was employed as personal physician to the Venetian consul. His time there enabled him to undertake extensive studies of local flora and fauna, with a particular interest in plants with medicinal qualities. He was aware of Prospero Alpini's work, having edited a new edition of his book in 1640 and having, two years earlier, published comments on it. Interestingly, in the course of these comments, he makes a distinction between a drink that was made from the husks of the coffee berries and one that was made from the beans themselves. He was enthusiastic about coffee:

Not only in Egypt is coffee in much request, but in almost all the other provinces of the Turkish Empire. Whence it comes to pass that it is dear even in the Levant and scarce among the Europeans, who by that means are deprived of a very wholesome liquor.

He also points out that in Cairo at the time there were two or three thousand coffee houses where 'some did begin to put sugar in their coffee to correct the bitterness of it, and others made sugar-plums of the berries'.

So, Venice was probably the place where Italy's first cup of coffee was drunk and the first berries were imported, in all likelihood, by a member of the prominent Venetian family, the Mocenigos. The head of the family was a trader who had made his fortune by importing spices and other exotic goods from the East. Initially, coffee was very expensive and was used purely for medicinal purposes. It was being sold by apothecaries by about 1630, as Vesling records: '...the first step it made from the cabinets of the curious, as an exotic seed, being into the apothecaries' shops as a drug'. The beverage then began to be sold by lemonade-vendors who listed it amongst the various drinks they peddled. By 1645, it was being drunk everywhere in Italy.

It is uncertain where and when the first coffee shop appeared but there is a record of one opening under the Procuratie Nuove (New Procuracies), the residencies of the procurators on the southern side of St Mark's Square in Venice in 1683. In 1720, Floriano Francesconi opened what is today reckoned to be the world's oldest coffee house still trading. Initially called *Venezia Trionfante* – Venice Triumphant – it is better known now as Caffè Florian, operating from the same location. Francesconi was a well-connected Venetian personage, a friend of the Italian Neoclassical sculptor, Antonio Canova (1757-1822), and his Caffè Florian became the hub of social and cultural life in the city. Venetians who were going on journeys would leave their cards and itineraries with him and those newly arrived in the city would head there to get themselves up-to-date on what was happening and find out who they should meet while they were visiting. The English essayist and social commentator, William Hazlitt (1778-1830), wrote that Francesconi 'long concentrated in himself a knowledge more varied and multifarious than that possessed by any individual before or since'. Hazlitt wrote on the subject of coffee:

Venetian coffee was said to surpass all others, and the article placed before his visitors by Florian was the best in Venice. Of some of the establishments as they then existed, Molmenti has supplied us with illustrations, in one of which Goldoni the dramatist [Carlo Goldoni (1707-93)] is represented as a visitor, and a female mendicant is soliciting alms. So cordial was the esteem of the great sculptor Canova for him, that when Florian was overtaken by gout, he made a model of his leg, that the poor fellow might be spared the anguish of fitting himself with boots. The friendship had begun when Canova was entering on his career, and he never forgot the substantial services which had been rendered to him in the hour of need.

Before long, every shop on Piazza San Marco in Venice was a Caffè and from the late seventeenth century until midway through the eighteenth, coffee houses sprang up across Italy. And, as always with coffee, revolutionary thoughts were never far away. The authorities maintained a watchful eye on Caffè Florian and other establishments. When some radical patrons of Marco Ancilloto's Caffè della Spaderia proposed opening a reading room in the establishment to help spread liberal ideas, the inquisitors sent someone round to inform Ancilloto that the first person to try to use the room should immediately present himself before their tribunal. In the face of such a daunting prospect, the idea was hurriedly shelved. However, the English agricultural and travel writer, Arthur Young (1741-1820), on a visit to Venice in 1788, described St Mark's Square and its plethora of coffee houses as the city's 'seat of government, of politics and of intrigue'.

Caffè Aurora opened in Venice in 1723, bringing a new type of coffee house. Located next to the campanile in the Procuratie Nuove, it had something of the Parisian coffee house about it, with an elaborate interior décor and high-quality fittings. Solid silver bowls, saucers, basins and plates were used and coffee was served in cups of the finest china. This drew a higher-class clientele and was quickly followed by the other similar Caffès in St Mark's Square.

Venetian coffee houses welcomed all, regardless of class

or status. In the morning they would be busy with lawyers, doctors, brokers and workers, getting their coffee fix before the start of the working day, or meeting to discuss business and other weighty matters. During the remainder of the day, they were frequented by the leisure classes, including women, who would often find a simple establishment with low ceilings, no windows and poor lighting. Smaller rooms were sometimes given over to gaming.

When coffee arrived in Rome, it is said to have caused a stir amongst some Roman Catholic priests who, in the manner of Muslim rulers and clerics, thought it should be banned. They petitioned Pope Clement VIII (1535-1605), claiming coffee to be the invention of Satan, insisting that the Prophet had allowed his followers – Muslims – to drink coffee after they had been forbidden from drinking wine. They had been forbidden from drinking wine, according to these priests, because it was used in Holy Communion. Thus, for Christians to drink coffee, they reasoned, was to fall into a trap set by the Devil. Intrigued by what they told him about coffee, Clement insisted that some be brewed and brought to him. Deciding that it had a pleasant aroma, he decided to sample a little. On drinking it, legend has it that he exclaimed: 'Why, this Satan's drink is so delicious that it would be a pity to let the infidels have exclusive use of it. We shall fool Satan by baptizing it, and making it a truly Christian beverage'.

The most famous Roman coffee house was Caffè Greco which was serving coffee by 1750. Greco was the favourite for a group of artists, sculptors and antiquarians who made their homes in Rome to serve the cultural needs of the young men undertaking the Grand Tour, the journey around the cultural centres of Europe that became an essential part of the lives of the elite young of Great Britain. These artists frequented the Greco's three small rooms but, following a disagreement, they decamped to a coffee house just up the street on the Piazza di Spagna that they turned into the Caffè degli Inglese – the English Coffee House. It was used by the Scottish biographer and diarist, James Boswell (1740-95), who had his mail sent there while he was visiting Rome. The young Welsh landscape painter, Thomas Jones (1742-1803), described the coffee house as being located 'in a filthy, vaulted room… painted with Sphinxes, Obelisks and Pyramids, from capricious designs of Piranesi, and fitter to adorn the inside of an Egyptian-Sepulchre than a room of social conversation'. On first setting foot in the place, he reckons to have encountered 18 old friends from London. He enjoyed the conviviality and the warmth of the Caffè degli Inglese, as a relief from the winter cold in his damp lodgings: '…seated around a brazier of hot embers placed in the Centre, we endeavoured to amuse ourselves for an hour or two over a Cup of Coffee or Glass of Punch and then grope our way home darkling, in Solitude and Silence'. Later, in the nineteenth century, Caffè Greco would once again become a meeting place for American, British, German and Danish artists.

In Milan, a philosophical and literary publication entitled *Il Caffè*, was founded by the economist, historian and philosopher, Count Pietro Verri (1728-97) and published between 1764 and 1766. It was so named because the count and his friends met at a coffee house in Milan owned by a Greek named Demetrio. Meanwhile, of the coffee houses opening across Italy, one of the most beautiful was the Caffè Pedrocchi in Padua. Work on it started in 1816 and it was fully open by 1831. Its rooms decorated in a variety of styles, it is acknowledged as one of the finest buildings erected in Italy during the nineteenth century. It played an important role during the 1848 riots against Habsburg rule and was frequented by a number of artists and writers, including Stendhal and Lord Byron. Florence and Genoa also saw the flourishing of coffee culture.

France's Love Affair with Coffee – the Early Years

France's first acquaintance with coffee can be attributed to three men – Jean-Baptiste Tavernier (1605-89), Jean de Thévenot (1633-67) and François Bernier (1620-88), three travellers who wrote about their experiences amongst the many different cultures they encountered.

Tavernier was a merchant in gems who reckons to have journeyed some 60,000 leagues (about 180,000 miles) during six journeys to Persia and India between 1630 and 1668. The French king, Louis XIV (r. 1643-1715), rewarded him handsomely, assuming the role of patron and funding his book, *Les Six Voyages de Jean-Baptiste Tavernier*, published in 1675. In it, Tavernier describes the coffee house and says that every Persian with leisure time repaired daily to it:

> The seats are plac'd as in so many Amphitheatres, and in the midst of every one stands a large vessel full of running Water, where with their Pipes be cleans'd when they are over foul.

It has been said that natural scientist and botanist, Jean de Thévenot, who travelled to the Near and Middle East between 1655 and 1659, was responsible for introducing coffee privately into Paris in 1657. In 1663, he once again set sail for the East, calling at Alexandria, Damascus and Aleppo and travelling through Mesopotamia. He reached Persia in August 1664 before spending five months in Isfahan in modern-day Iran. There, he met up with Jean-Baptiste Tavernier, journeying with him to Shiraz, Lar and Bander Abbas on the Persian Gulf with the intention of finding a passage to India. The Dutch were at the time making it difficult to travel and, although Tavernier was able to proceed, de Thévenot preferred to return to Shiraz. He eventually sailed for India, leaving Basra in November 1665. After travelling across India, he returned to Persia and, having been wounded by a pistol-shot, he died at Mianeh in that country in 1667. In his writings, he describes how the Turks made coffee:

> They have another drink in ordinary use. They call it *cahve* and take it all hours of the day. This drink is made

from a berry roasted in a pan or other utensil over the fire. They pound it into a very fine powder. When they wish to drink it, they take a boiler made expressly for the purpose, which they call an *ibrik*; and having filled it with water, they let it boil. When it boils, they add to about three cups of water a heaping spoonful of the powder; and when it boils, they remove it quickly from the fire, or sometimes they stir it, otherwise it would boil over, as it rises very quickly. When it has boiled up thus ten or twelve times, they pour it into porcelain cups, which they place upon a platter of painted wood and bring it to you thus boiling. One must drink it hot, but in several instalments, otherwise it is not good. One takes it in little swallows for fear of burning one's self – in such fashion that in a *cavekane* (so they call the places where it is sold ready prepared), one hears a pleasant little musical sucking sound… There are some who mix with it a small quantity of cloves and cardamom seeds; others add sugar.

The traveller and philosopher François Bernier, meanwhile, spent 12 years practising medicine at the court of the Mughal emperor, Aurangzeb (r. 1658-1707), bringing back information about this energising new beverage, although he promulgated some mis-information as well. Speaking to the English physician and naturalist Tancred Robinson (c. 1658-1748) in London in 1685, Bernier said that the coffee fruit was sown every year under trees, up which it climbed. Bernier, therefore, concluded wrongly, that it was a species of Convolvulus, 'a *Phaseolus*, or some other scandent [climbing] Legume'. Bernier also passed on to him the myth that coffee beans were always boiled by the Arabs before being sold in order to inhibit the possibility of their germination.

The first reference to coffee in France is probably to be found in a letter of 1596 that the Italian botanist and writer, Onorio Belli (1550-1603), sent to the French botanist and horticulturist, Charles de l'Écluse (1526-1609). He mentions 'seeds used by the Egyptians to make liquid they call *cave*'. French merchant, Pierre de la Roque, travelled with the French ambassador to Constantinople and, in 1644, brought back to Marseille not just coffee, but also 'all the little implements used about it in Turkey, which were then looked upon as great curiosities in France'. Amongst these were long-handled coffee pots – known as *finjans* – and embroidered muslin napkins.

People began to get used to coffee, especially those who had lived for a time in cultures where it was in everyday use. Around 1660, some Marseille merchants brought back a quantity of it from the Levant where they had been living and a short while later coffee was imported commercially from Egypt for the very first time. Merchants in Lyon followed suit and coffee began to be consumed in that city and in Marseille on a regular basis. In 1671, to serve the needs of French merchants who already knew of coffee from their travels, a coffee house was opened in Marseille, close to the Exchange, and it became a popular haunt of travellers and merchants.

As ever, as coffee surged in popularity, controversy

blossomed. Some doctors suggested that it was unhealthy for the natives of such a dry, hot country to consume the beverage and matters became quite heated between the opposing factions. In 1679, the doctors forced a student who was trying to gain admission to the College of Physicians to argue in support of their views in a debate in Marseille town hall about how harmful coffee was to the inhabitants of the city. The student described it as not comparable to wine, that it was a horrible foreign novelty, that it burned up the blood, created palsies, made people lose weight and that its consumption brought on impotence. Of course, this was all patently false and coffee, by this time, had become too popular to fall foul of such arrant nonsense. The coffee houses continued to do great business, to the extent that coffee beans began to be imported by the boatload from the Levant.

In 1699, Suleiman Aga, the Turkish ambassador to the court of King Louis XIV arrived at Versailles to be welcomed by the king. Allegedly, the monarch was offended by the fact that the ambassador turned up to meet him wearing only a simple woollen coat and hat and also did him the gross discourtesy of refusing to bow to him. The furious Louis banished him from Versailles, sending him to live in Paris instead. Suleiman had brought a quantity of coffee with him and began to introduce the beverage, made in the Turkish style, to Parisian society. He invited high-born Parisian society women to his home for extravagant 'coffee ceremonies' which were imitated by members of polite society across the capital. He instigated a fashion for what was known as 'Turquerie' – the imitation of aspects of Turkish art and culture – and Orientalism. Many Western European countries became fascinated by the exotic and relatively unknown culture of Turkey.

In 1672, an Armenian named Pasqua Rosée, of whom we will hear more, launched a coffee booth at the fair in the Saint-Germain quarter of the capital. Before long, coffee was being drunk in the French provinces and people were also brewing it at home. It was drunk by everyone for breakfast as well as after dinner and it became customary to offer it to visitors. A book on the subject of coffee, *The Most Excellent Virtues of the Mulberry, Called Coffee*, was published in Lyon in 1671 and Philippe Sylvestre Dufour (1622-87) published an authoritative work in 1684 – *Concerning the Use of Coffee, Tea, and Chocolate*. In 1715, Jean de la Roque's *Voyage de l'Arabie Heureuse* detailed the author's journey to the Yemen four years previously, providing a description of the coffee tree and the fruit that grew on it. He also wrote about the history of the beverage and how it first arrived in France. It was evident from his writings that the Arabs still believed that coffee grew only in Arabia.

In 1692, a Parisian banker, François Damame was given the sole licence to sell coffee in France. The edict declared:

His Majesty, after listening to the advice of the Council of State, has granted to Maître François Damame the exclusive privilege, for three years from January 1, 1692, of selling coffee, tea, chocolate, and the materials of which they are made; likewise cocoa and vanilla; in all the provinces, towns and domains of the realm of France.

The announcement went on to order all merchants and shopkeepers in possession of coffee in either powdered form or beans to send them to Damame's offices to be weighed, labelled, sealed and stored in warehouses. Those failing to do so were to be subject to a fine of '1500 livres'. Marseille and Rouen were listed as the only ports entitled to import coffee and only Damame had the authority to issue permits to move coffee. He was given the right to appoint employees to sell it. However, the price that was set for coffee turned out to be too high and consumption plummeted. Eighteen months after being granted this extraordinary monopoly, his finances in tatters, Damame requested of Louis XIV that he be released from it.

Gabriel de Clieu

After coffee emerged from the stranglehold of the Arabs and the Dutch proved that it could be grown elsewhere, gardens throughout Europe begged the Royal Physic Garden in Amsterdam for cuttings. Only one such request was granted. In 1714, the Dutch sent a cutting to the French king, Louis XIV, a keen gardener and amateur scientist. It seems strange that the Netherlands should do such a thing, given that France, along with England, was a great trading rival of the Dutch, but this plant would be one of the most significant in history, as it was the progenitor of coffee plants in the Caribbean, as well as in Central and South America.

The islands of the Caribbean, brutally denuded of their indigenous peoples long ago, were largely controlled by the French. The natives had been replaced by Huguenots – French Protestants – who had been forced to leave France when the king had revoked the Treaty of Nantes in 1685 that had given Protestants political and civil rights. They arrived in the Caribbean to work as indentured servants on the sugar and tobacco plantations. But on these plantations, there were also countless workers who had been given no such choice – slaves.

By this time coffee had become an everyday pleasure in Europe, made still more palatable by the addition of the sugar that was being imported from the plantations. The French were eager to capitalise on the popularity of the new beverage and the islands of the Caribbean looked as if they might give them the opportunity. All they had to do was convey a coffee plant 4,000 miles across the Atlantic but, at that time, that was easier said than done. With the winds and the salt of the sea-spray, and the lack of sunlight and warmth, plants intended to make the crossing had little chance of survival before the invention in 1829 of a glass terrarium, known as the Wardian Case, by the English doctor, Nathaniel Bagshaw Ward (1791-1868). There had been two previous attempts, both of which had failed, by the time Gabriel de Clieu (c. 1687-1774) decided to convey a cutting to the Caribbean.

De Clieu was a young gentleman from Normandy, born in a village not far from Dieppe. By 1720, he was serving as an infantry captain on the Caribbean island of Martinique. That year, he returned to France and while there he learned of the coffee cutting that had been sent to Louis XIV from the Netherlands that was being cultivated in Paris. He resolved to convey a cutting to Martinique in order to try to introduce the cultivation of coffee to the Caribbean. The difficulty he had, however, was in laying his hands on a cutting from that plant. It is suggested he got it through the good offices of a certain Monsieur de Chirac, a royal physician, who was persuaded to do so by the charms of a young noble lady of de Clieu's acquaintance.

The young naval officer boarded ship at Nantes on the west coast of France in 1723, his plant safely stowed in a box covered with a glass frame that would enable the sun's rays to be absorbed and the heat to be retained on cloudy days. It is said that there was a man on board who was keen to separate de Clieu from his plant but, despite dastardly attempts, he failed to do so. De Clieu recounted his travails in a letter to the publication, *L'Année Littérature*, detailing '...the infinite care that I was obliged to bestow upon this delicate plant during a long voyage, and the difficulties I had in saving it from the hands of a man who, basely jealous of the joy I was about to taste through being of service to my country, and being unable to get this coffee plant away from me, tore off a branch.' This was not his only worry. He was travelling on a merchant ship that encountered numerous difficulties on its voyage. It was almost captured by Tunisian pirates, was almost sunk by a violent tempest, and was then becalmed, which was worse, according to de Clieu, than either the pirates or the storm. They were forced to ration their drinking water for the remainder of the journey and incredibly, de Clieu made a great sacrifice to keep his coffee plant cutting alive: 'Water was lacking to such an extent,' he wrote, 'that for more than a month I was obliged to share the scanty ration of it assigned to me with this my coffee plant upon which my happiest hopes were founded and which was the source of my delight. It needed such succor the more in that it was extremely backward, being no larger than the slip of a pink.'

On arriving in Martinique, de Clieu remained concerned about the security of his small coffee tree. He planted it immediately in a part of his garden that he believed would be most suitable for it and surrounded it with thorn bushes to deter anyone from digging it up and making off with it. He resorted eventually to posting guards – probably slaves – to watch over it night and day until it reached maturity. He wrote how much he valued '...this precious plant which had become still more dear to me for the dangers it had run and the cares it had cost me.'

Guarded 24 hours a day by slaves, this one small plant would be the progenitor of most of the coffee trees in the Antilles. It would be responsible for the riches of most of the coffee barons on the wealthy estates of the West Indies and the regions that lined the Gulf of Mexico. De Clieu's tree produced its first harvest in 1726. Of these early days of coffee cultivation in the region, he wrote of a fortuitous weather event that made coffee all the more valuable and gave it a firm foothold in the region:

> Success exceeded my hopes. I gathered about two pounds of seed which I distributed among all those whom I thought most capable of giving the plants the care necessary to their prosperity. The first harvest was very abundant; with the second it was possible to extend the cultivation prodigiously, but what favored multiplication, most singularly, was the fact that two years afterward all the cocoa trees of the country, which were the resource and occupation of the people, were uprooted and totally destroyed by horrible tempests accompanied by an inundation which submerged all the land where these trees were planted, land which was at once made into coffee plantations by the natives. These did marvelously and enabled us to send plants to Santo Domingo, Guadeloupe, and other adjacent islands, where since that time they have been cultivated with the greatest success.

It is estimated that, by 1777, there were 18,791,680 coffee trees on Martinique.

De Clieu was appointed governor of Guadeloupe in 1737, retiring in 1752 with a pension of 6,000 francs. A year later, he re-entered service, but retired again seven years later. In 1750, he was made an honorary commander of the Royal and Military Order of Saint Louis, the prestigious French military honour that preceded the Légion d'Honneur. When he died in Paris at the age of 87, a Martinique newspaper paid tribute to his achievement:

> Honor to this brave man! He has deserved it from the people of two hemispheres. His name is worthy of a place beside that of Parmentier who carried to France the potato of Canada. These two men have rendered immense service to humanity, and their memory should never be forgotten – yet alas! Are they even remembered?

Early Parisian Coffee Houses

As we have already seen, coffee was introduced to Paris in 1657 by Jean de Thévenot, but once again it was not welcomed by all. About a dozen years later, the French aristocrat, the Marquise de Sévigné (1626-96), known as Madame de Sévigné, who is remembered for her witty and revealing letters, famously wrote: 'There are two things Frenchmen will never swallow – coffee and Racine's poetry'. Nonetheless, it is said that Louis XIV drank his first cup of coffee in 1664 and, as we have seen, the Turkish ambassador, Suleiman Aga, brought the beverage with him to Paris. Again as noted earlier, it was first sold to the general public at the Fair of Saint-Germain by Pasqua Rosée, an Armenian who had launched coffee in London more than 20 years previously (see Chapter 3). In 1672, Rosée opened a coffee house on the Quai de l'École, close to the Pont Neuf, in the centre of Paris, the first coffee shop in the capital. Sales were sluggish, Parisians still favouring wine and beer, but Rosée sent Turkish boys out into the streets with large, steaming jugs of coffee, heated by lamps, selling to passers-by and knocking on doors. Other men of Levantine origin sold coffee in the streets and in coffee shops – one called Joseph and another, Stephen, who hailed from Aleppo. The latter opened his establishment on Pont au Change and later relocated to the more salubrious Rue St André. In 1676, another Armenian, Maliban, opened a coffee house, initially in Rue de Bussy in the Saint-Germain area of the city but he could be found later in other locations. Such establishments appealed to the working classes and Jean de la Roque said of them that: 'Gentlemen and people of fashion were ashamed to go into those sort of publick-houses, where they smoked, and drank strong beer: besides, their coffee was none of the best, nor the customers served in the handsomest manner'. But, soon, more sophisticated coffee houses began to appear, equipped with tapestries, chandeliers, mirrors and marble tables. They began to be frequented by those higher up the social scale as well as by men of letters.

Coffee really took off in the reign of Louis XV (r. 1715-74) who, under the influence of his mistress, Madame du Barry (1743-93), championed the beverage, reportedly spending huge sums of money on it every year for his daughters.

The very first, peculiarly French, iteration of the coffee house appeared in 1689 when the Café de Procope was launched by an Italian former chef and lemonade-vendor.

Francesco Procopio Cutò, also known as Francesco Procopio dei Coltelli, (1651-1727), was born in Sicily and it is said that while he was still very young, he mixed snow with fruit juice and honey to make a type of sorbet which he sold. From this, he is said to have developed what we know as the gelato. He initially worked as a fisherman but also designed a machine that could produce gelato on a large scale.

Leaving Sicily, he travelled to France to sell his new product, training as a chef in the meantime. In Paris, he worked for Pasqua Rosée, selling refreshments from his kiosk at the annual Saint-Germain fair. Sales were poor, forcing Rosée to leave for London, giving the kiosk to Cutò who began to develop a drink made of lemonade ice. He was granted a special licence from Louis XIV to sell a range of refreshments as well as his fruit-based Italian gelatos which, until then, had been reserved for aristocrats and the elite. Before long, he added coffee to the menu, relocated to Rue de Tournon and, in 1686, to Rue des Fosses-Saint-Germain-des-Près. When, fortuitously, a year later, the Comédie Francaise opened in a theatre across the street, his café became the meeting place of choice for actors, writers, musicians, poets, dramatists and literary critics.

Cutò changed both his own name and the name of the café in 1702, making it more French. He became François Procope and his establishment became Café Procope, the name that it retains to this day. Everyone who was anyone met at Café Procope and the celebrated Enlightenment writer and philosopher, Voltaire (1694-1778), is said to have drunk 40 cups of coffee, laced with chocolate, there every day. French dramatist and writer, Louis-Sebastien Mercier wrote:

> All the works of this Paris-born writer seem to have been made for the capital. It was foremost in his mind when he wrote. While composing, he was looking towards the French Academy, the public of Comédie Française, the Café Procope, and a circle of young musketeers. He hardly ever had anything else in sight.

On 18 December 1752, the philosopher, writer and composer, Jean-Jacques Rousseau (1712-78) arrived in the café even before the end of the performance of his last play, *Narcisse*, letting everyone know that it was all so boring now that he had seen it performed. The compilers of the *Encyclopédie* which was published in France between 1751 and 1772, enjoyed a coffee there, as did such American luminaries of the age as Benjamin Franklin, John Paul Jones and Thomas Jefferson. During the French Revolution, the Phrygian cap, the soft conical cap with the apex bent over that became the symbol of liberty, was first displayed at the Café Procope. The Cordeliers Club, the revolutionary Society of the Friends of the Rights of Man and of the Citizen, met there and a number of the Revolution's main players, including Jean-Paul Marat (1743-93), Maximilien Robespierre (1758-94) and Georges Danton (1759-94) were patrons. Napoleon Bonaparte, while still an artillery officer in search of a commission, frequented the café, often playing chess at one of its tables. He is said to have once left his hat as security for an unpaid coffee bill. A plaque at the café details its illustrious history and claims it to be the oldest extant café in the world:

Café Procope. Here founded Procopio dei Coltelli in 1686 the oldest coffeehouse of the world and the most famous centre of the literary and philosophic life of the 18th and 19th centuries. It was frequented by La Fontaine, Voltaire and the Encyclopedistes: Benjamin Franklin, Danton, Marat, Robespierre, Napoleon Bonaparte, Balzac, Victor Hugo, Gambetta, Verlaine and Anatole France.

However, its claim to fame as the oldest coffee house is not entirely true. In fact, the original establishment closed its doors in 1872 and it became a private artists' club. When this proved unsuccessful, it returned to being Café Procope but then changed its name to Au Grand Soleil. It did not take long, however, for the new proprietor to realise the value of the old name and he rechristened it Café Procope, which it remains to this day.

An increasing number of cafés sprang up in Paris, described by de la Roque as:

Being thus changed into well furnished rooms ...[they] were crouded by gentlemen who came thither to drink coffee, and divert themselves with good company; and men of letters and the most serious persons, did not shun these meetings, where they might so conveniently confer on matters of learning, and what subjects they pleased, without any constraint or ceremony, and only by way of amusement.

As ever, the authorities were less enamoured of these new places of entertainment and leisure. In September 1685, the French Secretary of State, Jean-Baptiste Colbert, Marquis de Seignelay (1651-90), wrote to the Prefect of Police that, having learned that all sorts of people – especially foreigners – were in the habit of gathering in Parisian cafés, King Louis XIV wanted a report to be compiled on all the people who ran cafés and suggested that they be prohibited in future.

In 1673, in the midst of the popularity of several new alcoholic drinks – brandy, eau de vie and others – the right was given by the king to the recently instituted guild of *limonadiers* – lemonade vendors – to sell the new drinks as well as coffee and eaux de vie. This guild merged three years later with the guild of brandy merchants and distillers. Eau de vie proved to be a lucrative market and its success persuaded the *limonadiers* to change their businesses, to aim for a more upmarket clientele. This, in turn, led to a great change in Parisian cafés. They became principally vendors of alcoholic drinks and were not purely coffee houses. This French model of the coffee house/café, different to that of England and America where coffee houses were hubs for news and meeting places for businessmen and those seeking political debate, became the version that many European countries adopted. It was a mixture of the coffee house and the tavern and would soon be found all over the continent.

There were many celebrated cafés in Paris. Café de la

Régence began life in 1689 under another name, but after it was sold in 1718 to a Monsieur Leclerc, it was named in honour of Philippe II, Duke of Orléans (1674-1723) who acted as regent for Louis XV from 1715 until 1723. It became the meeting place for aristocrats and politicians after they had attended the royal court. The list of clients of the Régence reads like a history of French culture and politics. In 1867, a great chess tournament, the Great Tournament of Paris, was played there. It was won by Ignatz von Kolisch (1837-89) who beat such great luminaries of the contemporary chess world as Szymon Winawer (1838-1919) and Wilhelm Steinitz (1836-1900) who would go on to become the first undisputed World Chess Champion. In 1844, the writer of *Das Kapital* and *The Communist Manifesto*, Karl Marx (1818-83) met his fellow communist, Friedrich Engels (1820-95) for the first time in Café de la Régence. And in January 1906, Jean Sibelius is said to have improvised *A Prayer to God*, the main theme of the finale of his Third Symphony, at the café.

Celebrated French historian, Jules Michelet (1798-1874), said of the café culture of the first half of the eighteenth century:

> Paris became one vast café. Conversation in France was at its zenith. There were less eloquence and rhetoric than in '89. With the exception of Rousseau, there was no orator to cite. The intangible flow of wit was as spontaneous as possible. For this sparkling outburst there is no doubt that honour should be ascribed in part to the auspicious

revolution of the times, to the great event which created new customs, and even modified human temperament – the advent of coffee.

As increasing numbers of new cafés opened, their proprietors were forced to find ways to make their particular establishment stand out. Different types of cafés began to appear, such as the *café chantant* in which the clientele was entertained by monologues, songs, dances and plays – both dramas and farces. By the nineteenth century, many such concerns could be found on the Champs-Elysées, including the Eldorade, Alcazar d'Hiver, Scala, Gaieté, Concert de XIXme Siècle, Folies Bobino, Rambuteau, Concert Européen, amongst others.

Coffee in Holland

The Dutch traded with the Orient and with the Venetians which, therefore, brought them familiarity with coffee from an early date. They decided, however, not just to import coffee, but to grow it in their colonies and grab a large share of the increasingly lucrative coffee trade through the Dutch East India Company. This trading company had been founded by the Dutch government in 1602, initially to trade with the Indian Mughal Empire and with Southeast Asian countries where it was given a 21-year monopoly on the spice trade. Its directors selected Java as a likely location for the cultivation of coffee trees.

The first coffee to reach Holland was brought from Mocha in 1616 by the Dutch cloth merchant Pieter Van den Broecke (1585-1640), who was in the employ of the Dutch East India Company. Indeed, he was the very first Dutch person to drink coffee which he described as 'hot and black'. The first commercial shipment arrived in Amsterdam in 1640, four years before coffee arrived in France. The early pioneer of the beverage, Pasqua Rosée, pops up again at this point. Having opened London's first coffee house in 1652, he was selling coffee in Holland in 1664. The first coffee house was launched in The Hague around this time, with others following in Amsterdam and Haarlem.

In 1658, the Dutch swept the Portuguese out of Ceylon and began to cultivate coffee plants there. Coffee had already been introduced to the island by Arabs before the arrival of the Portuguese in 1505 and the Dutch began serious commercial cultivation in 1690. Java would become important in coffee cultivation after Nicolaes Witsen (1641-1717), mayor of Amsterdam and governor of the Dutch East India Company, in partnership with Adrian Van Ommen, commander of the Dutch garrison at Malabar in modern-day Indonesia, sent seedlings to Java in 1699. These initial plantings were swept away by flood water, but a second shipment was more successful and formed the basis for the lucrative coffee trade of the Dutch East Indies. In fact, Java would become a generic word by which coffee was fondly known. In 1706, the first shipment of coffee from Batavia (now Jakarta) arrived in Amsterdam, accompanied by a coffee plant that was destined for the city's botanical gardens.

This plant would be the one from which most coffee plants in the West Indies and the Americas were derived.

Coffee in Germany

As we have already seen, the first European mention of coffee in printed form was made by the German, Leonhard Rauwolf, in 1573. Other accounts of the beverage followed, such as that of the German Orientalist Adam Olearius (1599-1671) who travelled as secretary to merchants sent by the newly founded town of Friedrichstadt to Muscovy (modern-day Russia) and Persia in an attempt to secure Friedrichstadt as the terminus of an overland silk route. They left Hamburg in 1635 and returned to Germany in 1639 and, on his return, Olearius wrote of 'a certain black water' that the Persians called *cahwa*. It was, he wrote 'made of a fruit brought out of Egypt, and which is in colour like ordinary wheat, and in taste like Turkish wheat'. Similarly, in 1637, the German adventurer Johannes Albrecht von Mandelsloh (1616-44) wrote in his *Oriental Trip*, that the 'black water of the Persians called *Kahwe*... must be drunk hot'.

In 1670, coffee first appeared in Germany and it was drunk at the court of Frederick William, the Elector of Brandenburg (r. 1640-88) five years later. An English merchant opened Hamburg's first coffee house around 1679 and others followed across the country: Regensburg in 1689; Leipzig in 1694; Nuremberg in 1696; Stuttgart in 1712; Augsburg in 1713; and Berlin in 1721. For many years, all the coffee sold in northern German coffee houses was supplied by English merchants while the coffee for the south of the country came from Italy. In Berlin, the English Coffee House was opened by yet another Englishman. Other well-known establishments of the time were: the Royal, in Behrenstrasse; Widow Doebbert's coffee house in the Stechbahn; the City of Rome, in Unter-den-Linden; the Arnoldi, in Kronesstrasse; the Merck, in Taubenstrasse; and the Schmidt coffee house, in Poststrasse. During the reign of Frederick the Great (r. 1740-86), there were around a dozen coffee houses in the centre of Berlin and in the suburbs coffee was sold from tents. Writings on coffee began to appear. Theophilo Georgi published *The New and Curious Coffee House* in Leipzig in 1707. It described the doings of a group of men who visited the house of a well-off gentleman who lived on the outskirts of the city. In Nuremberg, in 1721, Leonhard Ferdinand Meisner published the first German treatise on coffee, tea and chocolate.

As had occurred elsewhere, however, the beverage soon ran into problems. The poor were told that coffee was not for them and doctors warned women that if they drank coffee they would be unable to bear children. Johann Sebastian Bach (1685-1750) wrote the 'Coffee Cantata' against such statements, sometime between 1732 and 1735. Essentially a miniature comic opera, it included lines – written by librettist Christian Friedrich Henrici (pen name Picander, 1700-64) – such as: 'If I couldn't, three times a day, be allowed to drink my little cup of coffee, in my anguish I will turn into a shriveled-up roast goat'. Frederick the Great was irritated by the fact that a great deal of money was being paid to foreign merchants for coffee beans and made efforts to restrict its consumption to the elite. In 1777, he published a manifesto that suggested his citizens should be drinking beer and not coffee:

> It is disgusting to notice the increase in the quantity of coffee used by my subjects, and the amount of money that goes out of the country in consequence. Everybody is using coffee. If possible, this must be prevented. My people must drink beer. His Majesty was brought up on beer, and so were his ancestors, and his officers. Many battles have been fought and won by soldiers nourished on beer; and the King does not believe that coffee-drinking soldiers can be depended upon to endure hardship or to beat his enemies in case of the occurrence of another war.

The love for coffee was too great, however, and it proved impossible for the royal stipulation to be maintained, even in a state as strict as Prussia. In 1781, therefore, Frederick took it a stage further, creating a state monopoly. In an ordinance entitled *Déclaration du Roi concernant la vente du café brûlé*, roasting of coffee beans anywhere but in royal roasting establishments was forbidden. The nobility were allocated special licences for roasting and, as they could only obtain beans from the government, Frederick made a lot of money, especially as the price was greatly increased. As the wealthy paraded their ability to roast coffee as if it was an honour bestowed upon them, the poor relied for a coffee-*like* fix on a range of substitutes – drinks made from wheat, corn, chicory and dried figs. If they did get their hands on some real coffee, they were in danger of being discovered by spies known as 'coffee-smellers' – often discharged wounded soldiers – who roamed the streets, noses twitching in search of the tell-tale aroma.

The Archbishop-Elector of Cologne, Maximilian Frederick (r. 1761-84) followed suit with a lofty pronouncement that was solemnly intoned from the region's pulpits:

> To our great displeasure we have learned that in our Duchy of Westphalia the misuse of the coffee beverage has become so extended that to counteract the evil we command that four weeks after the publication of this decree no one shall sell coffee roasted or not roasted under a fine of one hundred thaler, or two years in prison, for each offense. Every coffee-roasting and coffee-serving place shall be closed, and dealers and hotel-keepers are to get rid of their coffee supplies in four weeks. It is only permitted to obtain from the outside coffee for one's own consumption in lots of fifty pounds. House fathers and mothers shall not allow their work people, especially their washing and ironing women, to prepare coffee, or to allow it in any manner under a penalty of one hundred thaler. All officials and government employees, to avoid a penalty of one hundred gold florins, are called upon closely to follow and to keep a watchful eye over

this decree. To the one who reports such persons as act contrary to this decree shall be granted one-half of the said money fine with absolute silence as to his name.

The same measures were taken to uncover those breaking the rules, with coffee-smellers and people being encouraged to inform on their neighbours. Once again, the sole aim of the archbishop was to make money, as well as to ensure that those of lesser means were not able to enjoy a cup of coffee. Needless to say, the lure of coffee was too strong and the scheme was a flop. Meanwhile, Karl Alexander, Duke of Württemberg (r. 1684-1737), had a different approach. He sold the right to run coffee houses in his duchy to a corrupt Jewish banker, Joseph Seuss-Oppenheimer (1698-1738). Seuss-Oppenheimer then proceeded to sell the coffee houses and amassed a considerable fortune, possibly the first person to earn big money from coffee.

Soon, however, coffee had become woven into the fabric of German society and it remains, to this day, easily the country's favourite beverage.

Austria Rewards the Saviour of Vienna

The Ottoman Turks had already been repulsed by the Habsburg Empire a couple of times in the sixteenth century and, in 1683, a force of 300,000 troops, led by Grand Vizier Kara Mustafa Pasha (r. 1676-83) was once more at the gates of Vienna, besieging the city for two months. They were opposed by an allied force of Habsburg, German and Polish soldiers, led by John III Sobieski, King of Poland (r. 1674-96). The military governor of Vienna, Count Rudiger von Starhemberg (1638-1701), asked for a volunteer to carry a message through the Turkish lines to an army of 33,000 Austrians assembled behind the Turks. George Franz Kolschitzky (1640-94) stepped forward. Kolschitzky had lived for many years amongst the Turks and spoke their language, having previously worked as a translator for the Austrian Oriental Company. On 13 August, 1683, he famously donned a Turkish uniform, slipped undetected through the Turkish forces outside the city walls and reached the army of the Austrian Emperor Leopold (r. 1658-1705) which was encamped across the River Danube. Indeed, he made this perilous journey a number of times, swimming across the river on each occasion. Kolschitzky brought word back to the governor of Vienna that the king and Charles V, Duke of Lorraine (1643-90), who led the Emperor's army, would give the signal to attack the Turkish force from the summit of Mount Kahlenberg. The signal was duly given and they attacked on 12 September, routing the Turks who were forced to retreat, leaving behind 25,000 tents, 10,000 cattle, 5,000 camels, 100,000 bushels of grain, a large quantity of gold and a huge number of sacks filled with coffee beans. The Austrians were bemused, never having seen the beans before, and, when the spoils were divided between the various forces, no one wanted the coffee. Apart from Kolschitzky, that is. He was happy to take the sacks of unwanted beans, because, having lived in Turkey, he knew exactly what they were and he determined to make the Viennese get to know them, too. According to one story, he was also given a house where he established a café known as the Blue Bottle and he served coffee there for many years afterwards. The Viennese guild of coffee makers would later erect a statue in honour of Kolschitzky, as the patron saint of Viennese coffee houses.

To much of the world, the Viennese café became the archetypal coffee house. Amongst the best known is Café Sacher which has a recipe named after it – Sachertorte, a chocolate cake created in 1832 for the famous Austrian Chancellor, Prince Metternich (1773-1859). Another popular accompaniment to coffee in Vienna is the *kipfel*, a roll baked in a crescent shape, which may commemorate the Turkish siege in 1683 but, according to some sources, goes back further than that.

Coffee houses proliferated in Vienna. By 1839, there were 80 in the city and another 50 in the suburbs. Their popularity can be seen in this description by a tourist early in the eighteenth century:

The city of Vienna is filled with coffee houses, where the novelists or those who busy themselves with the newspapers delight to meet, to read the gazettes and discuss their contents. Some of these houses have a better reputation than others because such *zeitungs*-doctors gather there to pass most unhesitating judgment on the weightiest events, and to surpass all others in their opinions concerning political matters and considerations.

All this wins them such respect that many congregate there because of them, and to enrich their minds with inventions and foolishness which they immediately run through the city to bring to the ears of the said personalities. It is impossible to believe what freedom is permitted, in furnishing this gossip. They speak without reverence not only of the doings of generals and ministers of state, but also mix themselves in the life of the Kaiser (Emperor) himself.

'The history of coffee houses 'ere the invention of clubs, was that of the manners, the morals and the politics of a people.'

Benjamin Disraeli (1804-81), British Prime Minister

3

Coffee and the British

Early British References to Coffee

Although English travellers were as keen as anyone on the Continent to let people know about the new beverage from the East, the first reference to coffee in English was by a Dutch physician, Berent ten Broecke (1550-1633), who wrote under the name Bernardus Paludanus. Paludanus was professor of philosophy at the University of Leyden but had also travelled widely. In 1594, he helped compile a book about the travels of a Dutch merchant, Jan Huyghen van Linschoten (c. 1563-1611). Van Linschoten had travelled to the Portuguese colony of Goa on the west coast of India between 1583 and 1592. He wrote a book about his travels but he was also promoting the Far East which he believed to have huge commercial potential. While describing the food of Japan and, in particular, the Japanese tea ceremony, he includes some words on the subject of coffee, comparing Japanese tea and the coffee of the Turks:

The Turks holde almost the same manner of drinking of their Chaona, which they make of a certaine fruit, which is like unto the Bakelaer, and by the Egyptians called Bon or Ban: they take of this fruite one pound and a half, and roast them a little in the fire, and then sieth them in twentie poundes of water, till the half be consumed away: this drinke they take every morning fasting in their chambers, out of an earthen pot, being verie hote, as we doe here drink aqua composita in the morning: and they say it strengtheneth and maketh them warme, breaketh wind, and openeth any stopping.

The book gained a wide readership due to the wealth of commercial information it contained. It also came to the notice of well-known scientists of the day, such as Francis Bacon who looked into the physiological effects of the coffee bean. In 1599, English gentleman-adventurer, Sir Anthony Shirley (1565-1635), travelled from Venice to Persia in order to attempt to enlist the support of the Shah for the Christian princes against the Turks. The story of his journey, published in 1601, was written by one of his party, William Parry. It includes the first printed reference in English to a modern form of the word 'coffee' or in this case 'coffe'. He wrote:

They sit at their meat (which is served to them upon the ground) as Tailers sit upon their stalls, cross-legd; for most part, passing the day in banqueting and carowsing, until they surfet, drinking a certaine liquor, which they

74

do call *Coffe*, which is made of seede much like mustard seede, which will soone intoxicate the braine like our Metheglin [a type of mead].

Captain John Smith (c. 1580-1631), founder in 1607 of the Colony of Virginia, wrote of coffee in his 1630 book, *The True Travels, Adventure and Observations of Captain John Smith* saying that the Turks' best drink is 'coffa of a grain they call *coava*'. Samuel Purchas (1577-1626) wrote in *Purchas His Pilgrimes* (1607) about Arabs' 'best entertainment' – '…a china dish of *Coho*, a black, bitterish drinke, made of a berry like a bayberry, brought from Mecca, supped off hot, good for the head and stomache.'

William Biddulph, preacher to the Company of English Merchants, was the first Englishman to provide a detailed description of coffee and coffee houses as found in Turkey. It appeared in his book, *The Travels of Certayne Englishmen in Africa, Asia, etc… Begunne in 1600 and by some of them finished – this yeere 1608*:

Their most common drinke is Coffa, which is a blacke kinde of drinke, made of a kind of Pulse like Pease, called Coaua; which being grownd in the Mill, and boiled in water, they drinke it as hot as they can suffer it; which they finde to agree very well with them against their crudities, and feeding on hearbs and rawe meates…It is accounted a great curtesie amongst them to give unto their frends when they come to visit them, a Finion or Scudella of Coffa, which is more holesome than toothsome, for it causeth good concoction, and driveth away drowsinesse.

...Their Coffa houses are more common than Ale-houses in England; but they use not so much to sit in the houses, as on benches on both sides the streets, neere unto a Coffa house, every man with his Finionful; which being smoking hot, they use to put it to their Noses & Eares, and then sup it off by leasure, being full of idle and Ale-house talke whiles they are amongst themselves drinking it; if there be any news, it is talked of there.

English traveller, Edward Terry (1590-1660), wrote in 1606 that Indians drink:

...a liquor more wholesome than pleasant, they call coffee; made by a black Seed boyld in water, which turns it almost into the same colour, but doth very little alter the taste of the water, notwithstanding it is very good to help Digestion, to quicken the Spirits and to cleanse the Blood.

Like Biddulph, the Scottish traveller, William Lithgow (c. 1585-c. 1645) who walked from Paris to Jerusalem between 1609 and 1614, believed that the Turks treated coffee as a substitute for wine which the Koran forbade them from drinking. He wrote:

...the usual courtesie, they bestow on their friends, who visite them, is a Cup of Coffa, made of a kind of seed called Coava, and of a blackish colour; which they drinke so hote as possible they can, and is good to expell the crudity of raw meates, and hearbes, so much by them frequented. And those that cannot attaine to this liquor, must be contented with the cool streams of water.

As for the taste of the beverage, the poet, Sir George Sandys, who, in 1610, spent time in Turkey, Egypt and Palestine, was not at all keen. He described it as black as soot and not actually tasting much better than that! William Parry, who, as we have seen, was a member of the 1601 expedition to Persia led by Sir Anthony Shirley, suggested that to anyone who was not familiar with the drink, it tasted like medicine. Indeed, he failed to understand how anyone could enjoy it.

Both Biddulph and Sandys believed that coffee acted on the mind in a similar way to opium which they would also have encountered in Turkey. It 'driveth away drowsiness', Biddulph wrote and he added that it encouraged good conversation, just like opium. But, of course, while coffee kept people awake and gave them 'alacrity', opium did just the opposite.

Although Sir Francis Bacon and the English philosopher and humourist Robert Burton (1577-1640) both wrote in praise of the Turkish drink, *coffa*, writers later began to suggest that they had found evidence in the works of Arab authors that coffee could create a melancholy state of mind and that its consumption encouraged headaches.

The English Orientalist Edward Pococke stated that the Turk 'would drink it for livelinesse sake, and to discusse slothfulnesse… let him use much sweet meates with it, and oyle of pistaccioes, and butter'. He even ascribed alarming, although misguided side effects: 'Some drink it with milk, but it is an error, and such as may bring in danger of the leprosy'.

One would presume that such a wide range of references to coffee would imply that it must have been introduced to England in the first quarter of the seventeenth century, but the earliest reference to its actual consumption appears in the *Diary and Correspondence of John Evelyn, F.R.S.* The year in question was 1637 and he writes:

> There came from the college (Baliol, Oxford) one Nathaniel Conopios, out of Greece, from Cyrill, the Patriarch of Constantinople, who, returning many years after was made (as I understand) Bishop of Smyrna. He was the first I ever saw drink coffee: which custom came not into England till thirty years thereafter.

However, it did not take 30 years before the beverage was available from a coffee house, as the first one opened in 1651. A Jewish Lebanese entrepreneur, named Jacob, opened the first English coffee house, called the Angel, at the junction of Queen's Lane and The High in Oxford. Jacob would later move to Old Southampton Buildings in London. A second, the Queen's Lane Coffee House – which is still in existence – followed three years later, launched by Cirques Jobson, and in 1655, an apothecary named Arthur Tillyard opened another adjacent to All Souls College. Tillyard had been persuaded to open his coffee house by the popularity of the beverage amongst the town's student population. A club consisting of admirers of the future King Charles II (r. 1660-85) began to meet at Tillyard's coffee house. Anthony Wood (1632-95), an antiquarian of the time, wrote in his diary that '[Tillyard] was encouraged to do so by som Royallists, now living in Oxon, and by others who esteem'd themselves either *virtuosi* or *wits*'. These latter characters were those who dabbled with the new experimental science for whom Tillyard provided a room in his coffee shop. The Chemical Club, as it was known, would evolve into the Royal Society, the United Kingdom's national academy of sciences. Other coffee establishments followed in Oxford and by the time of the Restoration, there were a number in the city. The lawyer and biographer Roger North (1653-1734) wrote of how it was a 'Custom, after Chapel, to repair to one or the other of the Coffee-houses (for there are diverse) where Hours are spent in talking; and less profitable reading of News Papers, of which Swarms are continually supplied from London'.

By the end of the 1660s, coffee houses were open in places like Yarmouth, Harwich and York. John Kimber's Coffee-House was operating in Bristol at the sign of the Elephant, and Lionell Newman had opened one in Dublin by 1664, as evidenced by a token he issued that depicted an Ottoman sultan on one side. In 1673, John Row was pouring coffee at his establishment near the Parliament House in Edinburgh. That same year, Glasgow was also introduced to the joys of the beverage by Colonel Walter Whitford to whom Glasgow council generously gave a 19-year monopoly on the sale of coffee. His coffee room, Glasgow's first, opened on the corner of Trongate and Saltmarket.

The coffee house arrived in Cambridge, too. But the authorities quickly became concerned by the possibility that coffee would distract the students from their studies. A statute was passed in 1664 that promised punishment for all students who went to the coffee house without an accompanying tutor. Within a few years, however, the coffee house had become an important part of university life in Cambridge.

Coffee pioneer, Pasqua Rosée, whom we already met in Paris, is another name that figures in the story of the beverage's arrival in Britain. In 1652, he opened London's first coffee house. He had been born into the ethnic Greek community in the republic of Ragusa before moving to Smyrna in Western Armenia where he was employed as a manservant by English merchant, Daniel Edwards. Having travelled to Britain with Edwards, he opened his establishment in St Michael's Alley, Cornhill. The sign that hung outside was a portrait of Rosée himself. Rosée later moved to Paris where, as we have seen, he opened the first coffee house in the French capital in 1672.

London's First Coffee Houses

As we have seen, Pasqua Rosée came to London as a manservant employed by a merchant named Daniel Edwards. In 1652, Rosée opened the first coffee house in London, in St Michael's Alley, in Cornhill in the City of London. He established it in partnership with the coachman of one of Edwards' sons-in-law, Christopher Bowman. But the partnership did not last, the two men quarrelling, and Rosée was left as sole proprietor of the coffee house. Bowman, meanwhile, went off to pitch a tent in St Michael's Churchyard from which he sold coffee in direct competition with his former partner. A local worthy wrote some verses about the threat to Pasqua's business. He titled his poem 'To Pasqua Rosée, at the Sign of his own Head and half his Body in St Michael's Alley, next the first Coffee-Tent in London':

> Were not the fountain of my
> Tears Each day exhausted by the steam
> Of your Coffee, no doubt appears
> But they would swell to such a stream
> As could admit of no restriction
> To see, poor Pasqua, thy Affliction.
>
> What! Pasqua, you at first did broach
> This Nectar for the publick Good,
> Must you call Kitt down from the Coach
> To drive a Trade he understood

No more than you did then your creed,
Or he doth now to write or read?

Pull Courage, Pasqua, fear no Harms
From the besieging Foe;
Make good your Ground, stand to your Arms,
Hold out this summer, and then tho'
He'll storm, he'll not prevail – your Face
Shall give the Coffee Pot the chace.

Another version of the story claims that Bowman was brought into the enterprise because, as the coffee house became increasingly popular, local publicans petitioned the Lord Mayor that Rosée was a foreigner and not a freeman and, therefore, had no legal right to be running such an establishment. Thus, Bowman was brought in to legitimise the operation. The very first advertising handbill for coffee in Britain was made by the enterprising Rosée and now sits in the British Museum. It reads in part: 'The Vertue of the COFFEE Drink First publiquely made and sold in England, by Pasqua Rosée... in St Michaels Alley in Cornhill... at the Signe of his own Head'. It was in a London publication – the *Publick Adviser* – that the world's first-ever newspaper advertisement for coffee appeared. The original is preserved in the British Museum. It was published on 26 May 1657, and read:

In *Bartholomew Lane* on the back side of the Old Exchange, the drink called *Coffee* (which is a very wholsom and Physical drink, having many excellent vertues, closes the Orifice of the Stomack, fortifies the heat within, helpeth Digestion, quickneth the Spirits, maketh the heart lightsom, is good against Eye-sores, Coughs, or Colds, Rhumes, Consumptions, Head-ach, Dropsie, Gout, Scurvy, Kings Evil, and many others) is to be sold both in the morning, and at three of the clock in the afternoon.

When coffee first arrived in England, a duty of four pence was imposed on every gallon that was made and sold and Parliament classed it with what it termed as 'other outlandish drinks'. At the same time, it was being sold in powder form at the Turk's Head coffee house for four shillings to six shillings and eight pence a pound. Pounded in a mortar, it sold for two shillings; the East India berry went for one shilling and sixpence; and the 'right Turkie berry' for three shillings. Beans – known as 'ungarbled' coffee – went for less. Instructions were provided.

In 1663, all coffee houses in England were required to be licensed, the licence costing about 12 pence. If a coffee house proprietor neglected to obtain a licence, he was subject to a fine of five pounds for every month his establishment had been unlicensed. Meanwhile, the first royal warrant for coffee was issued by Charles II (r. 1660-85) to a Scotsman, Alexander Man, who began to advertise himself as 'coffee man to Charles II'.

Some British coffee houses initially had specific tables for specific subjects, such as politics, literature or games.

Still later, rooms were allocated according to subjects to be discussed. Gradually, products other than coffee began to be sold, such as sherbert, chocolate and tea. By about 1669, some were also offering ale and beer. However, the devastating Great Fire that destroyed large parts of London in 1666, obviously put paid to many coffee houses. One that survived was the Rainbow, London's second coffee house, opened in 1657, and owned by James Farr. It was used as a meeting place by freemasons and later as an information centre by the French Huguenots, Protestants who had been forced to flee France by Louis XIV's 1685 Edict of Fontainebleau, which removed their civil and political rights. Farr was one of the earliest to use a new marketing gimmick – a token that had the value of a halfpenny and could be redeemed by a customer at a coffee house. Christopher Bowman's coffee house, run after the Great Fire by George Backler, was another to issue tokens. The earliest is said to be one issued by the Solyman in Ivy Lane in 1663. Arguably the most famous of the early coffee house keepers was Thomas Garraway whose establishment was located in Exchange Alley from around 1668 or 1670 until the late nineteenth century. An advertisement in the political journal, *Mercurius Politicus*, would suggest that Garraway was the first person in England to sell leaf tea.

It should not be forgotten that coffee houses were very sociable venues and many visitors to London were of the opinion that they were, in fact, the best thing about the capital. Everyone – except women, of course – was welcome and they were very different to taverns and inns. They were much calmer places and customers did not have to endure the noise and occasional violence of those establishments. They very much reflected the changes in society, the emergence of a middle class and the desire to spend leisure time in a sober environment in pursuit of debate and the exploration of ideas. Furthermore, drinking coffee sharpened the mind somewhat and kept the drinker awake, while continued consumption of alcohol often led to stupor and aggression.

While, unlike on the continent, women were not permitted to be customers of coffee houses, they were often run by a coffee woman. Opposite the Houses of Parliament stood one such place known simply as Alice's after the proprietor. In the London City *Quaeries* of 1660 there is listed 'a she-coffee merchant' by the name of Mary Stringar who is known to have run an establishment in Little Trinity Lane, in the City, close to the Thames. Another, Anne Blunt, was running one of the Turk's Head coffee houses in Cannon Street in 1672 and Mary Long was involved with the Rose coffee house in Bridge Street, Covent Garden.

In those times, travel across town could be dangerous and the coffee house provided a very convenient place to meet and conduct business. And there was no pressure to buy. In fact, one cup could easily be made to last for an entire day. This was especially useful in the cold winter weather when the coffee house could provide heat and shelter. Seventeenth century London coffee houses became known as 'penny universities' because of the level of debate and conversation that could be found in them. The entrance fee was a penny, over and above the two pence for a cup of coffee or tea. This money went towards newspapers to be read while drinking and to cover the cost of lighting the establishment. Of course, there was also the added expense of a tip.

Events at the end of the Republic in England in 1659 consolidated the coffee house as a hub of political intrigue but not everyone was in favour of its role in the politics of the day. For example, the clergyman and scientific writer John Beale (1608-83) disapproved. He suggested that the coffee bean's popularity meant that money was being diverted from the British economy into the coffers of 'our foreign brethren'. He wrote: '[the] Coffa-drinke will growe into generall use having already obtain such a general reception by young & old in our Innes of Courts; & I should rather wish our supply from our owne plantations, than from Turkye'.

Meanwhile, some wondered whether coffee would agree with the English. In *England's Monarchy Asserted and Proved to be the Freest State, and the Best Commonwelth Throughout the World*, the writer wonders 'Whether Coffee, Sherbet, that came from Turky, Chocolate much used by the Jews, Brosa by the Muscovites, Ta and Tee, and such other new-fangled drinks, will agree with the Constitutions of our English bodies'. But there were also moral slanders attributed to coffee and coffee houses. In his *Select City Queries: Discovering several Cheats, Abuses and Subtilties of the City bawds, Whores and Trapanners*, published in 1660, the pseudonymous Mercurius Philalethes asks 'whether Mrs *Huzzy*, a late Coffee-merchant, has not more rooms to let than Beds to lie in; and whether the East India Merchant could lodge in hers (during her husband's absence) and *Margery Speights* blinde Chapel at one and the same time'. In such musings, the coffee house is projected as a house of ill repute. There is little doubt that, with its opportunities for radical talk, politicking and its transgressive coffee-women, it was firmly at the centre of the impulse for social change in England.

It was a time before the delivery of mail had been organised in any official way and the coffee houses linked up with the Post Office to convey letters and newspapers to customers who would collect them when they visited. Coffee houses were also places where you could find out the latest hot news. 'Runners' would turn up with information about the day's major events, whether it was news of a battle or a political scandal.

Indeed, it was a time when the provision of news was a relative novelty and the coffee house became a news hub. The English had emerged from the Interregnum with a hunger for salacious gossip about the mistresses of Charles II, rumours about republican uprisings and happenings abroad. The result was a public that was increasingly vocal in its opinions and more politically aware. For the powers-that-be, this was, of course, anathema, because as far as they were concerned, the only news of any value was news about the king, his court and his government, provided by those very same bodies. Other news, not provided from these sources was brushed aside as fake, even if it was true. Those rules did not apply in coffee houses, however, where people continued to discuss the latest happenings in the world.

There was also some printed news. Samuel Pepys (1633-1703), the great English diarist, writes about reading an account of a scandalous trial in the 'news-booke'. Pepys, who worked at the Naval Office, also found that he learned more about naval matters in the coffee house than he did at work or from Whitehall. One estimate suggests that around 30 per cent of all the visits he made to the coffee house resulted in news that he believed to be of sufficient import to write about it in his diary. A fine example of this was the day that he listened to the musings on the possibilities of 'a Dutch war' from a Baltic merchant and navy contractor, Captain George Cocke.

Charles II Suppresses Coffee

Of course, coffee houses also provided centres for sedition and rebellious plotting. Indeed, many Protestant plots against the monarchy in the 1660s were hatched in the dark corners of coffee houses and were a direct result of the socialising such enterprises fostered. While paying a visit to London in 1664, the French doctor and philosopher Samuel de Sorbière (1615-70) noted that the coffee houses were a-buzz with complaints about high taxes and regrets that

Cromwell's regime was no more. In the same year, Charles II's Secretary of State, Henry Bennet, Earl of Arlington (1618-85), was given information relating to rebellious discussions that had been taking place at a coffee house in Lothbury in the City. A certain Major Holmes, who had been an officer in Cromwell's army, had been arguing in favour of 'liberty of conscience'. He claimed that his fellow rebels would obtain weapons from Holland, through a merchant named Benbow. Thus it was argued that there was a link between the news promulgated in coffee houses and sedition. By around 1666, the king was becoming very concerned about such political discussion in coffee houses, especially criticism of his conduct during the Great Fire of London. He ordered his Lord Chancellor, Edward Hyde, the Earl of Clarendon (1609-74), to deal with it. Clarendon said that Charles:

> ...complained very much of the Licence that was assumed in the Coffee-houses, which were the Places where the boldest Calumnies and Scandals were raised, and discoursed amongst a People who knew not each other, and came together only for that Communication, and from thence were propagated over the kingdom; and mentioned some particular Rumours which had been lately dispersed from the Fountains.

Clarendon carried out an investigation that concluded that men in coffee houses 'generally believed that [they] had a Charter of Privilege to speak what They would, without being in Danger to be called in Question'. He advised the King to take action by issuing a proclamation to suppress the coffee houses, but nothing came of this and they continued as before.

Around that time, the only regulation regarding coffee houses was the Excise Act 1660, in which the excise tax was extended to coffee. The tax on coffee was set at 4 pence a gallon, while the tax on tea and chocolate was set at 8 pence, rising to 6 pence and 16 pence respectively in 1670. The way this worked was that the tax was levied at the point of manufacture or consumption. This made it relatively easy to evade paying the tax as it was difficult to measure. Recognising this, the government introduced an Additional Excise Act in 1663. This forced coffee house operators to pay a security bond to the excise for which they received a certificate. The certificate allowed them to apply for a licence from the magistrates without which they could not trade. The fine levied for each month without a licence was £5, equivalent to around £1,000 in today's money.

These moves did little to prevent coffee houses being a bastion of free speech, speech that was often critical of the King and his government and, therefore, a proclamation was issued in June 1672 aiming to 'Restrain the Spreading of False News, and Licentious Talking of Matters of State and Government', as its title said. It further claimed that:

...men have assumed to themselves a liberty, not onely in Coffee-houses, but in other Places and Meetings, both publick and private, to censure and defame the proceedings of State, by speaking evil of things they understand not, and endeavouring to create and nourish an universal Jealousie and Dissatisfaction in the minds of all his Majesties good subjects.

People were urged to report anyone criticising the government to Privy Councillors or a Justice of the Peace within 24 hours, but it achieved nothing. May 1674 brought another proclamation threatening those who were 'Seditiously inclined', but once again, nothing changed. At the same time, however, the state used coffee houses to gather intelligence, with correspondents placed within them to report back on public opinion. One such was the Yarmouth publican, Richard Bower who was a correspondent, or spy, for the office of Sir Joseph Williamson, Secretary of State for the Northern Department (1633-1701). Yarmouth was, at the time, a hotbed of Nonconformist Protestantism and it was Bower's job to report by letter to the government on the political mood of the town. Bower used his wife to gain information by having her run a coffee house. She was able to report back on not only the gossip she heard, but also the prevailing political mood and even shipping movements to Holland.

So, like Eastern potentates before him, Charles II moved to suppress the consumption of coffee. His judges, however, were unable to agree whether the banning of coffee would be constitutional and some suggested that it would be foolish to ban it in view of the substantial revenue the government derived from it. Politician Sir William Coventry (c. 1628-86) reminded Charles that the king actually owed coffee houses a debt of gratitude as it was in them that his supporters had been able to convene and plan his restoration to the throne when they were unable to speak freely elsewhere. Coventry added that, anyway, a ban on coffee would be almost impossible to police. Finally, the judges came out somewhat reluctantly in favour of the king's plan, declaring:

> Retailing coffee might be an innocent trade, as it might be exercised; but as it is used at present, in the nature of a common assembly, to discourse of matters of State, news and great Persons, as they are Nurseries of Idleness and Pragmaticalness, and hinder the expence of our native Provisions, they might be thought common nuisances.

Opposition to the King was growing and becoming increasingly coherent. The noblemen who opposed the government, the Duke of Buckingham (1628-87) and the Earl of Shaftesbury (1621-83) became known as the Country Party, and thought of themselves as patriots, defenders of England. They were nicknamed the Whigs by their enemies and they adopted the name themselves. The court party, that of the King was associated with the high life and Whitehall and St James, while the opposition met in bookshops, taverns, at the Exchange and in private houses, but increasingly became associated with coffee houses. In the Parliament of 1675, there were a number of actions that attempted to restrict people's liberty. The Test Act, for instance, forced all holders of political office to swear that they would never take up arms against the King and that they would not try to change the government. If it had been passed it would have created nothing short of an absolute monarchy, but towards the end of October Parliament fought against it, leading to the prorogation of Parliament by Charles until 15 February 1677, a gap of 15 months before it was allowed to sit again. Meanwhile, coffee houses continued to breed what the government newsletter writers described as the 'most indecent, scandalous and seditious discourses'. On 29 December 1675, therefore, in the absence of Parliament, Charles issued *A Proclamation for the Suppression of Coffee Houses* in which he detailed his reasons for the suppression:

Whereas it is most apparent that the multitude of Coffee Houses of late years set up and kept within this kingdom, the dominion of Wales, and town of Berwick-upon-Tweed, and the great resort of Idle and disaffected persons to them, have produced very evil and dangerous effects; as well for that many tradesmen and others, do herein mispend much of their time, which might and probably would be employed in and about their Lawful Calling and Affairs; but also, for that in such houses... divers false, malitious and scandalous reports are devised and spread abroad to the Defamation of his Majestie's

Government, and to the Disturbance of the Peace and Quiet of the Realm...

In this proclamation, coffee house operators were ordered to stop retailing 'coffee, chocolate, sherbet and tea' on 10 January 1676. Naturally, this could have spelled disaster for the coffee men but it also appeared to many to be not just the suppression of coffee, but the suppression of liberty and free speech. The proclamation appeared in *The London Gazette* the following day and was to be implemented by the recall of the licences that had been issued by magistrates under the previous excise legislation. Coffee house owners would thereafter be prosecuted for trading without a licence. The suppression of coffee generated a great deal of outrage. A private newsletter of 1 January 1676 talked of the 'mutinous condition in this towne upon the account of coffee houses... The suppression of them will prove a tryall of skyll. All wits are at worke to elude ye Proclamation'. But, for the government to back down would cause it grievous harm, as the newsletter went on to make clear: '...if the government shew itself to feare the people I suspect the people will hardly feare the Government'.

The coffee men were not without support. Some, such as Thomas Garraway of the Exchange, had become wealthy and their wealth and family connections had given them an entrée into the elite. Garraway's cousin, for instance, was William Garraway, MP for Chichester. Many also acknowledged the commercial importance of the coffee houses, especially in the City of London. A petition to the Privy Council was drawn up and presented on 7 January 1676 by Garraway and another coffee man, a Mr Taylor. To the Chancellor of the Exchequer, Sir John Duncombe (1622-87), they stated their credentials as legal coffee sellers who paid their tax which, they reminded him, went straight into the King's coffers. The proclamation would bring an end to this. Not only that, the coffee men would suffer hardship and would be left with large stocks of coffee that would result in its price collapsing. They asked for a chance to sell their coffee but also to continue trading. They were ushered into the Privy Council room to deliver their petition to the King and his councillors. Later that day, after much debate in secret, the Privy Council announced that the proclamation was to be rescinded. The coffee shops could remain open for six months during which they would have a chance to prove their loyalty. Charles issued a counter-proclamation stating that he was reversing his decision out of what he called 'princely consideration and royal compassion'.

During the session, Taylor had proposed that coffee men would be willing to accept stricter regulation. He suggested that the excise men should issue licences only to men who were loyal and that the coffee men should inform of any seditious utterances in their establishments. In effect, he was offering them up as government spies. This led the Attorney General, Sir William Jones (1631-82), to list the standards that would be required of coffee houses and their owners:

Expedients:

1. Not in common rooms.

2. Good behaviour from the master of the house &c. to the extent of those of alehouses.

3. On any information found of words spoken &c. in any coffee house and not discovered by the master whether he were present or no, he to forfeit his recognizance.

4. Printed or written libels &c., letters &c. that are publicly spread or uttered in their house, the master to be answerable on bond.

On 8 January 1676, the *Additional Proclamation Concerning Coffee Houses* was published, giving the coffee men permission to trade until 24 June 1676. The coffee sellers' acknowledgement of the 'Miscarriages and Abuses committed in such Coffee-houses', and their promise of taking 'utmost Care and endeavor to prevent the like happening in the future' were incorporated in the proclamation. To ensure their good behavior, they had to put up £500 as surety. In addition, a £20 reward was offered for the discovery of printing presses and the writers of pieces critical of the King or his government. In the end, Charles realised he had bitten off more than he could chew and withdrew gracefully. The coffee houses continued trading and the ban on them was never enforced. They continued to be centres for debate and opposition and Shaftesbury and Buckingham were happy to continue using them as meeting places. They launched a 'pamphlet war', circulating their pamphlets around coffee houses and, in the summer of 1676, they both moved to the City for easier access to the Exchange and the area's other coffee houses. They were now aiming at gaining support from merchants, Protestant radicals and erstwhile republicans, widening the appeal of their party.

Francis Jenks (c. 1640-86), a linen draper in the City, was arrested and prosecuted for an anti-government speech he had made in June 1676, demanding an election for a new Parliament and the coffee houses were full of disquiet about it. On 14 September, the Duke of Buckingham met a group of men in an upstairs room at Garraway's Coffee House. Amongst those present were the republican lawyer, politician, soldier and former Leveller, Sir John Wildman (1621-93), who had been involved in several anti-government plots in the previous decade and the City goldsmith, financier, politician and alderman Edward Backwell (1618-83), one of the richest men in the country. Such a meeting involving an important republican and a City luminary suggested that the opposition was beginning to make progress and the public nature of it suggested that they were feeling politically stronger. The Duke is said to have raised his cup of tea to a new Parliament '...and to all those honest gentlemen of it that would give the King no money'. He was overheard by a government spy and a report of the meeting could be found next day in the newsletter issued by Williamson's Letter Office:

The Duke of Buckingham was last night in ye great Coffee house in the City in an excellent talking temper where he had a very full audience, before which he declared himself freely & aloud without enjoyning any secrecy that he was absolutely for a new parliament upon which subject he enlarg'd himself very openly & with liberty & plainness enough in conscience.

Of course, Garraway should have reported the incident to the Secretary of State's office but he claimed that on the night in question, he was in Edmonton, a village to the north of London and did not return until late that night. When he enquired of his staff what had been going on, none of them had heard anything. The evening had created uproar, however, and Garraway quickly realised that he was in danger of losing his coffee house and perhaps even his liberty. Therefore, he found a witness who had been at a different table in the same room as the Duke that night and who claimed to have heard nothing seditious. Garraway passed this information to Williamson's office. He was believed and the danger was averted. It is worth pointing out, however, that other coffee house proprietors were less fortunate than him. Nonetheless, it was apparent that coffee houses had made themselves synonymous with the British tradition of free speech.

It is almost impossible to know exactly how many coffee houses existed in London at the end of the seventeenth century, but it is estimated that there were perhaps around 2,000. They were now looked upon more kindly by the government, and four years after the Glorious Revolution of 1688 that replaced James II as king with William III of

Orange and his wife, Mary II, the punitive import duties on coffee were halved 'for the greater encouragement and advancement of trade and the greater importation of the said respective goods and services'.

One Man's Coffee House Life – Samuel Pepys

In the marvellous *Diaries of Samuel Pepys*, kept by him from 1660 to 1669, but not published until the nineteenth century, we first encounter a detailed account of one individual's coffee house history at the time when the beverage was first becoming popular. Of course, Pepys discussed everything in his diaries, from money to his most secret thoughts but he also details 99 coffee house visits between 1 January 1660 and 31 May 1669.

When his diary opens, Pepys, who worked as Clerk of the Acts to the Navy Board, was a frequenter of the tavern and only rarely visited the coffee house. However, around 1663, it became a big part of his life. He would visit one two or three times a week, depending on how much free time he had. To take one week in December 1663 as an example, he visited a coffee house three times, usually the one in Exchange Alley in the City of London. He describes how on Saturday 26 December he 'sat long in good discourse with some gentlemen regarding the Roman Empire'. On the Wednesday that followed, he could be found in the coffee house with a couple of Fellows of the Royal Society – Captain John Gaunt and scientist and philosopher Sir

William Petty (1623-87) – 'with whom I talked and so did many, almost the whole house there' on the subject of Petty's invention of a double-hulled sailing vessel. Next day, he was back 'and sat an hour or two at the Coffee, hearing some simple discourse about Quakers being charmed by a string about their wrists'.

Pepys loved the sociability of the coffee house. His diary makes clear that he enjoyed the company of the men he met there and the fellowship they offered. He listed their names so that if he met them again he would remember them. 'I find much pleasure' in the coffee house, he wrote, 'through the diversity of company – and discourse'. He also benefited professionally from friendships he formed with his superiors from the Navy Office who also frequented the establishments. In addition, he made the acquaintance of merchants, contractors, scientists, scholars and men who were associated with his patron, Edward Montagu, Earl of Sandwich (1625-72), a cousin of his father.

Pepys had ambitions, entertaining dreams of advancement, of being knighted and of riding in his own coach, but he realised that in order to be a great man, it was important that he behave like one. That is why he stopped visiting the tavern with its loutish connotations. Not only did drinking too much make him less efficient at work, but he was associating with the wrong kind of men. Great men did not drink in the public house. Looks were important and he began to spend more on clothes and threw lavish dinner parties at his house. He decided that the coffee house was the place for him to be seen, where he could meet the types of men who would help him to make progress in society as well as in his career. John Phillips (1631-1706), the nephew and secretary of the great poet, John Milton (1608-74), remarked several years later that the coffee house was indeed a 'happy Invention' for businessmen, 'for to drink in Taverns was scandalous, to be seen in an Ale-house more unseeming; but to sit idling away their Time in a Coffee-house... that's an Employment without the Verge of Reprehension'. Pepys adopted the coffee house with enthusiasm. In his diary, he relates how he went twice in one day and drank coffee 'till I was almost sick'.

He visited 'the Coffee-house in Exchange-ally' sometimes in the company of a friend or business associate, sometimes for a meeting with a specific person and often just on the off-chance of encountering someone or overhearing interesting conversation or news. He was particularly interested in meeting merchants because their information about the City of London could be of practical use to him in his job. Navy contracts were of particular interest, given his duties at the Navy Office. All this worked for him as his job as Clerk of the Acts changed from merely administrative tasks to the negotiation of contracts and the transaction of deals with suppliers. Indeed, he became wealthy from the bribes and backhanders he received in his work as a result of frequenting the coffee house. This, in turn, led to social advancement and enhanced contacts with members of the royal court. These meant the coffee house was no longer important to him and by 1665 he had given up visiting Exchange Alley.

Brewing and Drinking Coffee in the Seventeenth Century

It has to be remembered that hot beverages were not entirely new. There had been hot drinks before – the British climate made them a necessity – but they were caudles (recipes based on milk and eggs and/or various other ingredients such as wine, wheat starch, raisins and sugar); possets (milk curdled with wine or ale, often spiced – later a cream, sugar and citrus-based confection); and punches. There were also heated wines and various spirits spiced up with butter and cream. In the 1660s, the aroma and taste of coffee were strange things, indeed. 'Newfangled, Abominable, Heathenish Liquour', as the *Women's Petition Against Coffee* described it. There were insults a-plenty – 'thick as puddle-water'; 'tasting like boiled Soot'; 'made with the scent of old crusts, and shreads of leather burn'd and beaten to a powder'; 'black, nasty, Hel-burnt Liquor'; 'a syrup of Soot, or Essence of old Shoes'; 'a foreign Fart'; 'a Satanic Tipple'; 'the Sister of the common Sewer'; and perhaps most graphic of all, taken from *The Character of a Coffee-House, with the Symptomes of a Town-Wit* of 1673, 'that Witches tipple out of dead men's skulls, when they ratifie to Beelzebub their Sacramental Vows'.

Of course, it was all new to people, but it may well have not tasted terribly good. There was a requirement at the time for it to have a bitter flavour that could make it astringent and even medicinal in taste. It also had an effect on people and it was hard to discern whether it was the taste or that effect that made the beverage desirable. Other drinks of the period, rivals to coffee such as wine, beer and spirits, were subject to dilution in order to make the supply of them last longer. Spices and peppers were sometimes added to give them an edge and fruit and sugar were introduced to make them sweet and easier to drink. Coffee, on the other hand, was enjoyed most when it was pungent and strongly flavoured.

One of the most important tasks of the coffee-man would have been the roasting of his coffee beans. The beans would have been 'green' although, in reality, they would have been a dull, whitish-grey colour. In that condition, they could last a couple of years before being roasted. That timescale allowed them to travel from the coffee bush to the markets in Turkey or Egypt and then onwards to London. Once roasted, the beans would have to be ground and used within a few weeks.

There was, and is, an art to the roasting of coffee beans. They have to be exposed to heat for a certain length of time during which the bean undergoes a complex chemical transformation, in which the volatile oils that lend it its flavour and distinctive aroma are brought out. As they are heated in the roaster the beans crackle and pop, drying as the moisture inside them is forced out. At the same time they grow bigger, their volume increasing by at least 50 per cent. A chemical process called pyrolysis or volatisation occurs when the temperature inside the beans reaches between 185 and 240 degrees centigrade. During this process, complex chemical substances are broken down into simpler ones. At the same time, the sugars in the beans caramelise and the volatile oils intensify. The bean also becomes darker in colour. The longer the roasting, the darker the colour and the oilier the beans. Roast for too long, however, and the sugars and the oils will burn. To stop the process the beans need to be removed from the roaster and allowed to cool rapidly. Using modern equipment, the process lasts no more than a few minutes and different grades of roast can be achieved. This was not, however, something that could be done in the seventeenth century.

The early coffee men will often have been trained by Turks, but, in the beginning, roasting was done both in coffee houses and at home simply by holding a pan filled with beans over a fire. The pan would have been modelled on the Turkish version – a long-handled vessel with a tight-fitting lid that had a revolving mechanism connected to a paddle inside the lid. This was used to stir the beans as they roasted and prevent them from burning. Larger roasters consisted of a rotating drum that was turned by the use of a long handle over a fire pit. By the 1690s, a business developed, selling roasted coffee to coffee houses. One famous name involved in this was Thomas Twining (1675-1741), founder of the Twinings tea company, who, at the time, was the owner of Tom's Coffee House in Devereux Court, in the Temple area of London, close to the City. Some people liked to roast their own coffee beans at home. In July 1714, Jonathan Swift (1667-1745), the poet and Dean of St Patrick's Cathedral in Dublin, entertained fellow poet Alexander Pope (1688-1744) in his lodgings while on one of his frequent visits to London. Pope notes that, 'There was likewise a Side Board of Coffee which the Dean roasted with his own hands in an engine for that purpose, his Landlady attending, all the while that office was performing.'

An English doctor who was living in Bremen in the 1670s provided instructions as to how to make coffee powder:

Take any quantity of ye Coffee berry you please & put into a frying pan or like & hould it over an easy fire keeping it continually stirring so it burns not[.] the berry at first is white & after some drying will burne browne & at length be black[.] when you have thus well dryed it all the brownest of ye berry be turned in to perfect black then beat it in a morter & sift it through a fine sive & take ye quantity as above mentioned.

Coffee in those days was far from what would be expected by the modern imbiber. Hand-stirred beans will inevitably not be roasted evenly, and, if the beans are roasted over a coal or charcoal fire, the result will be a drink that is decidedly smoky. The volatile oils will not develop fully in under-roasted beans, resulting in a drink with a nutty, bread-like flavour and no aroma. Beans that are roasted too much will become black and burned and the coffee from these beans is likely to be sooty and taste of carbon. Again, there will be a distinct lack of powerful aroma.

The French traveller and champion of coffee, Jean de

Thévenot described how it was done in the *cave-hahe* of Ottoman Turkey:

> When they have a mind to drink of [coffee], they take a copper Pot, made purposely, which they call Ibrick, and having filled it with Water, make it boyl; when it boyls, they put in this Powder, to the proportion of a good spoonful for three Dishes or Cups full of Water, and having let all boyl together, they snatch it quickly off the fire, or stir it, else it would run all over, for it rises very fast.

The liquid was then poured into a cup or bowl, leaving the grainy residue in the pot. For Levantines, however, the secret of coffee lay in its freshness. They tried, therefore, to reduce the time between roasting, grinding and preparing. That having been done, the drink was supposed to be drunk immediately. Coffee houses in Damascus in the seventeenth century were continuously roasting and grinding coffee beans in order to retain the beans' freshness. Leaving the beans aside for any time in the process ruined the flavour of the drink. In England, it would appear that often all that mattered was the clarity of the drink. One recipe recommends leaving the coffee grounds to settle in the liquid after it has been boiled. Quality was sometimes not an issue. The ambassador to the Ottoman Empire, Sir John Finch (1626-82), stated in 1678 that what he termed ordinary people should be satisfied with using coffee grounds to make their coffee while 'Gentlemen' should always be served coffee made with freshly ground powder.

Coffee-making would not change until the eighteenth century, when the French, around 1710, came up with an innovative new method. Coffee that had been freshly roasted and ground was put into a cloth bag and boiling water was poured over this. The bag was then allowed to steep in it to infuse. This method was supposed to ensure that the drink was not impaired by grounds but, as the bag remained in the coffee for a while, it did little to improve flavour.

The early nineteenth century added a screw to the process that could be used to press down on the bag and extract as much flavour as possible from it. The more familiar drip method was also introduced. Employed mainly in the home, it involved pouring boiling water on compressed coffee grounds and letting them infuse with the water before allowing them to drip into a pot below through a filter. This retained the grounds and let through the water. Interestingly, all these methods were aimed purely at making the coffee look clear and had little to do with making it taste better.

While coffee was still something of a novelty, it was almost always drunk black and unadulterated. No sugar or milk was added to it. In fact, adding sugar was such a novelty that Samuel Pepys, having been served coffee with sugar in it in 1664, at the house of Vice Admiral Sir John Mennes (1599-1671), made mention of it in his diary. Sugar, which was extremely expensive at the time, was mostly added to coffee in the domestic situation and rarely in coffee houses. At the time, milk was not something healthy adults drank, and was considered fit only for children and those in poor health. It was, therefore, added to coffee for purely medicinal purposes. An example of this thinking can be found in Laurence Sterne's novel *Tristram Shandy*, in which the eponymous hero consumes a drink he describes as 'milk coffee', claiming that it was 'good for a consumption'. The way it was made was to boil the water and the milk together.

Finjans or *fincans* were the small ceramic dishes used for drinking coffee in the Ottoman Empire, cheaply produced and made of rough, red earthenware clay. These were covered in a white slip, or coating and a simple lead glaze was added to ensure that they were liquid-proof. They were light and easily broken which was why they had to be cheaply produced. They were held delicately using the thumb and the forefinger, between the bottom and the rim. Occasionally, they would have an accompanying flat dish to sit on, an early form of saucer. Of course, more elaborate coffee sets were produced with matching cups and pots. Pottery produced in Iznik, near Istanbul and at Kutahya in western Turkey and Damascus was beaten only in quality by the finest Chinese porcelain and some was imported into England, finding a home in large houses. Some 'Turkey dishes' could also be found in taverns and restaurants in England but, more commonly, the dishes used for drinking coffee were of Oriental origin. By the late seventeenth century, coarse, English-made, earthenware cups were on sale, made by London potteries and by the 1690s, a coffee mug, not unlike the modern iteration, was being made and sold.

The Miracle Drink

Coffee was ascribed miraculous properties by all kinds of people, from quacks to those who knew no better. Some lauded it, giving it healing qualities, while others damned it as little better than poison. The distinguished Oxford physician and founding member of the Royal Society, Dr Thomas Willis (1621-75), often prescribed a trip to the coffee house rather than the apothecary. It was claimed by many that it could cure drunkenness and even opponents of the beverage agreed with this. This particular power was celebrated in the song, *The Rebellious Antidote*:

> Come, Frantick Fools, leave off your Drunken fits.
> Obsequious be and I'll recall your Wits,
> From perfect Madness to a modest Strain
> For farthings four I'll fetch you back again,
> Enable all your mene with tricks of State,
> Enter and sip and then attend your Fate;
> Come Drunk or Sober, for a gentle Fee,
> Come n'er so Mad, I'll your Physician be.

Someone suggested that coffee could act as a good deodorant, while another said that had its properties been known in 1665, it would have been useful against the Great Plague of London in which 100,000 died in just 18 months. It was also recommended for use against the plague in the 1665 book, *Advice Against the Plague*, by the physician Gideon Harvey (1636/7-1702).

In *Pharmaceutice Rationalis* of 1674, Dr Willis supported both sides of the coin. On the one hand, he said that it was a risky drink that engendered listlessness and even paralysis. It could be dangerous, he claimed, for the heart and might create trembling in the limbs of a drinker. But, he believed that, if drunk carefully, it could provide benefits: 'being daily drunk it wonderfully clears and enlightens each part of the Soul and disperses all the clouds of every function'. Others such as Dr Daniel Duncan (1649-1735) of the University of Montpellier occupied the middle ground. In his *Wholesome Advice against the Abuse of Hot Liqueurs*, he claimed that coffee was neither poison nor panacea and the celebrated, pioneering English physician, George Cheyne (1672-1743) agreed.

Between the Restoration of the Stuart monarchy in 1660 and 1675, a number of pamphlets discussing coffee houses were published. *A Cup of Coffee: or, Coffee in its Colours*, published in 1663, described coffee as a 'loathsome potion'. In 1674, *The Women's Petition against Coffee, representing to public consideration the grand inconveniences accruing to their sex from the excessive use of the drying and enfeebling Liquor* was published, claiming that coffee made men impotent – as 'unfruitful as the deserts where that unhappy berry is said to be bought'. A response to it appeared in the same year, in the form of *The Men's Answer to the Women's Petition Against Coffee, vindicating… their liquor, from the undeserved aspersion lately cast upon them, in their scandalous pamphlet.*

Coffee's effect on male virility was first suggested by the Danish doctor, Simon Paulli (1603-80) professor of botany, anatomy and surgery at Copenhagen University. Writing about tobacco and tea, Paulli was scathing about coffee which he called 'cahvvae acqua'. He claimed that it 'surprisingly effeminates both the Minds and Bodies of the Persians'. As for European men, he insisted that it made them like eunuchs, 'incapable of propagating their Species…' He argued that male consumers of coffee may still be able to ejaculate, but their semen will have lost its power to generate new life. His thinking was derived from the observations of Adam Olearius who, as we have seen, travelled to Muscovy and Persia between 1635 and 1639. In Persia in 1637, he observed that coffee was used as a contraceptive by Persian men due to the 'Cooling quality' they thought it possessed. They believed that it 'allays the Natural heat… and would avoid the charge of having many Children'.

Others argued that coffee had other qualities. In 1771, a French doctor claimed that coffee could cause nymphomania, as it stimulated women's erotic imaginings. On the other hand, the German physician Samuel Hahnemann, the creator of homeopathy, blamed coffee for masturbation – 'the monster of nature, that hollow-eyed ghost, onanism, is generally concealed behind the coffee-table'. Of course, there is absolutely no evidence that coffee plays a part in any of these indulgences and conditions and, in fact, more recent research has postulated that coffee may increase sperm mobility, thereby increasing male fertility.

In 1671, a Syrian living in Rome, published a treatise in Latin on the health-giving properties of coffee. Antonio Fausto Naironi (c. 1635-1707) had travelled widely in the Ottoman Empire in the 1650s and was well placed to write about the West's involvement with coffee, including the 'discovery' of the coffee bean by Europeans such as Johannes Cotovicus, Prospero Alpini, Johann Vesling and Pietro della Valle. Naironi was a champion of the beverage but he was unsure of its medical properties, and whether it was hot or cold in terms of the humours. (Humourism was a medical system created by the Ancient Greeks and Romans that detailed the make-up and workings of the human body.) Although his medical analysis of coffee was decidedly lacking in substance, his work remained influential in the science of coffee for the next 100 years, circulating widely around Europe. It was an indication of the curiosity that existed about the beverage and its effect on the human body and psyche.

Thomas Willis, mentioned earlier, was one of the Royal Society's most eminent natural philosophers and was also a practitioner of new types of medicine. While remaining an adherent to the old methods, he also involved himself in more experimental science, analysing skilfully the physiological effects of his treatments. He recommended coffee as a treatment for what he described as 'sleepy Distempers'. And, while still recommending bloodletting and purging, the old methods, as a cure for persistent drowsiness, he also prescribed, 'At eight of the Clock of the Morning, and at five in the Afternoon... a draught of coffee, or the Liquor prepared of that Berry'. In his posthumously published book, *The London Practice of Physick*, of 1685, Willis recommends coffee for treating 'Head-aches, Giddiness [and] the Lethargy'. Drunk daily, he claims, 'it wonderfully clears and enlightens each part of the Soul, and disperses all the Clouds of every function'.

There were those in England who believed that coffee was a bad thing because it would undermine the sale of English ale. That, in turn, would mean the demand for English grain which was the primary ingredient of ale and beer would be reduced and would have a detrimental effect on the British economy. Others complained that people were spending too much time in coffee houses, drinking and talking when they should have been at work.

Coffee house proprietors were keen to promote the therapeutic qualities of their beverage. Coffee, according to them, was a panacea, as described in a handbill that the Rainbow Coffee-House in Fleet Street had printed and distributed:

The quality of this drink, is cold and dry; and though it be a drier, yet it neither heats, nor Inflames more than a hot Posset.

It so closeth the Orifice of the Stomach, and fortifies the heat within, that it is very good to help digestion, and therefore of great use to be taken about three or four of the Clock in the afternoon, as well as in the morning.

It is very good against sore Eyes, and the better, if you hold your head over it, and take in the Steam that way.

It suppresseth fumes exceedingly, and therefore good against the Headach, and will very much stop any Defluxion of Rhumes, that distil from the Head upon the Stomach, and so prevent, and help Consumptions, and the Cough of the Lungs.

It is excellent to prevent and cure the Dropsy, Gout, and the Scurvy.

It is known by experience to be better than any other drying Drink for people in years, or Children that have any running Humours upon them, as the King's evil. &c.

It is very good to prevent Miscarryings in Child-bearing Women.

It is a most excellent remedy against the spleen, Hypochondriack Windes, or the like.

It will prevent drowsiness, and make one fit for business, if one have occasion to watch; and therefore you are not to Drink of it after Supper, unless you intend to be watchful, for it will hinder sleep for three or four hours.

It is to be observed that in Turkey, where this is generally drunk, that they are not troubled with the Stone, Gout, Dropsie, or Scurvy; and that their Skins are exceeding clear and white. It is neither Laxative nor Restringent.

Lloyd's Coffee House

Edward Lloyd (c. 1648-1713) is believed to have been from Canterbury in Kent but moved to London with his wife, Abigail, around 1680 just after the death of their son. The City of London in the late seventeenth century was concerned with two things – shipping and finance – and business for these all took place in the small area of the capital between the Tower of London and Thames Street which was close to the Navy Office in Seething Lane, the office responsible for the day-to-day civil administration of the British Royal Navy. As we have seen, each coffee house catered for a specific special interest and, when he opened his coffee house on Tower Street, now Great Tower Street, Lloyd immediately began to attract a clientele that had an interest in maritime business. Ship's captains, ship owners and merchants who used the sea to transport their goods all met at Lloyd's to discuss maritime insurance and shipbroking as well as foreign trade. These dealings would lead to the eventual establishment of Lloyd's of London and Lloyd's Register of Shipping.

Lloyd soon realised that these various types of people who shared the same interest had a need for information and he began to supply it from his coffee house, publishing a regular sheet, *Lloyd's News*, that contained up-to-date bulletins about shipping schedules, insurance arrangements, cargoes and word of what was happening abroad. He even set up a network of correspondents who kept his customers in touch with events that impacted upon ports across Europe.

In 1691, with business booming, Edward Lloyd moved his coffee house to 16 Lombard Street, an ideal position just a few minutes' walk from the Royal Exchange, the centre for commerce in the City of London. It was also the centre of the merchants' quarter. Lloyd installed a pulpit in the coffee shop from which maritime auction prices and the latest shipping news were announced. The coffee house, with its sanded floor and staff of three men and two women, sold tea, sherbet and a fruit punch as well as coffee and there was a plentiful supply of pens, ink and writing paper for patrons.

Candle auctions were commonly held at Lloyd's. These were auctions that began with the lighting of a candle and ended when the candle flame expired. Thus, no one knew exactly when the auction would end, providing no opportunity, therefore, for last-second bids. Candle auctions are mentioned in the records of the House of Lords in 1641, but by the time of Lloyd's had largely fallen out of use. They were still used occasionally at Lloyd's, however, in the sale of ships and other items. Lots we know of that were sold in such a way, include 'a parcel of Turkish coffee' and '53 hogshead of extraordinary neat Red French wines'.

Edward Lloyd became a man of substance. He was elected as a sidesman – a greeter of the congregation – at his local church, St Mary Woolnoth and also became a Constable and Questman, which meant he was a member of an early form of police force or neighbourhood watch. He was also proposed as a councillor but was not elected due to his ill health. In early 1713, Lloyd wrote a will that assigned the lease of his coffee house to his head waiter, William Newton who was due to marry Lloyd's 19-year-old daughter, Handy, a few days later. Two weeks after that, 'the Coffee-Man on Lombard Street', as one newspaper described him in an obituary, died. His astonishing legacy lived on, however, in the institution that still bears his name – the insurance market known as Lloyd's of London.

William Newton died just a year after Lloyd, and Handy married Samuel Sheppard. When they died, the coffee house was left to Sheppard's sister, Elizabeth, and her husband, Thomas Jemson who, in 1734, founded *Lloyd's List*, which, like *Lloyd's News*, provided customers and others with weekly shipping news. It was one of the world's oldest continuously running journals when it published its final print edition in 2013, issue number 60,850. It now exists only in digital form. Insurance was negotiated in the coffee house until 1774 when those involved formed a committee and moved to the Royal Exchange as the Society of Lloyd's.

The Demise of the Coffee House

Samuel Pepys wrote that 'the bitter black drink called coffee' brought together all classes and kinds of men. Specific groups of men favoured specific coffee houses. The political parties of their day – the Whigs and the Tories – each had coffee houses that they favoured and much intrigue was carried out in those places. Intrigue of a religious nature was more likely to be found in coffee houses close to cathedrals, such as the St Paul's Coffee House. These would later evolve into clubs in some instances, particular buildings wherein men with shared interests could meet. A few became elite clubs such as the Athenaeum on Pall Mall which opened its doors in 1824. Entry to such establishments was by membership only and sometimes that membership was difficult to obtain. The various services that coffee houses had once provided were now the province of specialist service providers. For instance, whereas people used to collect their mail from the coffee house, the postal system now began to deliver letters and packages direct to homes. Coffee houses were no longer the source of news as newspapers were being published and distributed by new modes of transport and sold in newsagent shops. Insurance companies, once run from coffee houses such as Edward Lloyd's, were now wealthy and successful enough to work out of their own offices.

The nature of the coffee houses changed and they began increasingly to resemble taverns. At the end of the eighteenth century, there were as many clubs as there had been coffee houses in the early decades of the century. They had a brief revival as places where men could go to read newspapers, as observed by Sir Walter Besant:

> They were then frequented by men who came, not to talk, but to read; the smaller tradesmen and the better class of mechanic now came to the coffee-house, called for a cup of coffee, and with it the daily paper, which they could not afford to take in. Every coffee-house took three or four papers; there seems to have been in this latter phase of the once social institution no general conversation. The coffee-house as a place of resort and conversation gradually declined; one can hardly say why, except that all human institutions do decay. Perhaps manners declined; the leaders in literature ceased to be seen there; the city clerk began to crowd in; the tavern and the club drew men from the coffee-house.

The rise in popularity of the rival beverage tea also impacted coffee houses. Tea had become Britain's favourite drink and it could be brewed at home where it was mostly consumed. People were encouraged to drink it, making more money for the British East India Company which found tea considerably more profitable than coffee. The fact that tea could be consumed at home in a family setting, rather than in a coffee house where conspiracies were fomented and political unrest could be encouraged, worked in its favour. Wives were happy at the prospect of keeping a watchful eye on their husbands. Tea also had a less enervating effect upon the brain and was more liable to put consumers to sleep than to make them excitable in the way that coffee could. Twinings went so far as to open the first tea shop in 1717. Unlike coffee shops, it was designed to cater for ladies of fashion, permitting them to combine shopping and socialising.

The decline began to accelerate in the late eighteenth century. A number limped on into the early years of the nineteenth century, especially in the more 'artistic' parts of a city as meeting places for the cultural elite, but they had mostly lost their allure and their novelty. People increasingly drank both coffee and tea at home which negated the need to go to a specific place for that pleasure. Men would rather go to their clubs to exchange views with like-minded people, to debate and discuss or to make useful business connections. And so, coffee houses became chop houses – small restaurants serving individual portions of meat which were known as chops – or taverns, selling alcoholic drinks.

Coffee Knowledge

By around 1670, as we have seen, coffee was everywhere. Large quantities of it were brought to London and then distributed to coffee houses or to other English cities and even exported to other countries in Europe. Still, however, its origins – the plant from which it was derived – remained largely unknown. The familiar old tales were told about it but the accounts of travellers were inconsistent and no one could be entirely certain whether it was grown on a tree, a bush, a low shrub or a vine. There was also the matter of whether the coffee bean could be best described as a bean, a nut, a berry or a fruit.

It was not until 1693 that the English first got their hands on a specimen. A 'dryed Branch' was brought back from Mocha in Yemen and was handed over to a young botanist, Hans Sloane (1660-1753) of the Royal Society. Sloane's description of this specimen, preserved to this day in his herbarium at the Natural History Museum in London, is the first comprehensive botanical description of coffee. It became the definitive work and was relied upon throughout the eighteenth century. However, they still did not have in their possession a live tree which meant nothing could be said for certain about the cultivation of the coffee plant. For that to happen, they would have to rely on a coffee tree that was in the possession of another country.

That country was the Netherlands. The Dutch were far ahead of the other European powers in their cultivation of coffee. As we have seen, the Arabs jealously guarded their coffee plants, but in 1696, the Dutch had stolen some saplings from them in Yemen and sent them to Batavia (now Java) in the Dutch East Indies. To their delight, they discovered that the plant adapted wonderfully to conditions there and thrived. A living specimen was then sent to the Amsterdam Physic Garden where botanists kept it, under tight security, in a hothouse constructed specially for it. The English botanist and apothecary, James Petiver (c.1665-c.1718), wondered at the plant on a visit to the garden in 1711 and encouraged another English botanist, Richard Bradley

(1688-1732), to go and smuggle a cutting back to England. This was planted and cultivated under glass in a nursery in Hoxton owned by a man named Thomas Fairfax. In the meantime, a specimen had also been donated to the Royal Physic Garden in Paris. These specimens, in Amsterdam, Paris and London, would be used to spread cultivation of the coffee plant to the colonies of Britain, the Netherlands and France.

In 1737, coffee was described in accordance with his system of binomial nomenclature by the esteemed Swedish botanist, Carl Linnaeus (1707-78). Classified in the *Rubiceae* family, as a separate genus *Coffea*, it had just one known species at the time – *Arabica*. Its full name was *Coffea Arabica* Linnaeus. Of course, since then, more than 100 species of coffee have been found. These are of many disparate varieties, from small shrubs to trees that grow to more than 30 feet high. The most common is *Coffea Canephora* (var. Rustica) which was taken from Zaire to Brussels around 1900. Now widely cultivated around the world, it is well-known for its heavy crops and particularly large berries.

Coffee in the Colonies

The demand for coffee in England, France and the Netherlands led to a need for a reliable and constant supply of the bean. The problem was that it was still available only from Mocha and Yemen and supplies from these sources were dependent upon the whim of the caliphate. If the caliph decided one day that he no longer wished to supply the nations of the West with the means to brew their favourite beverage, there was no recourse to other sources.

The main European traders in coffee were the English and the Dutch whose East India Companies facilitated the movement of goods from the East to the West. They used trans-shipment ports in Gujarat or Malabar to purchase their coffee stocks, using the huge warehouses they had at their trading posts in those ports to stockpile it. The market for coffee was growing inexorably, however, and it became necessary to find more direct sources. As well as protecting supply, purchasing straight from the actual growers of the coffee bushes would also help them to maintain control over pricing. As can be imagined, however, Europeans were distrusted in Yemen. This was, in part, due to the hostility that had always existed between Muslims and Christians but it was also because of the activities of the ships owned by European merchants. They had been known very often to use the threat of violence in order to obtain better trading terms. Nonetheless, the Europeans had to understand that they would always operate at a disadvantage in the Red Sea trading region.

India provided the solution they were looking for. Legend had it that the coffee plant had been brought to the subcontinent in the sixteenth century by Baba Budan, a Sufi holy man, but it seems more likely that others were responsible for introducing coffee plants – perhaps sailors, merchants or sufis who travelled back and forward to Yemen, bringing back seeds in order to satisfy their craving for coffee. It gradually became clear to Dutch merchants that, given the right conditions, they could grow their own coffee beans, far from the eyes of the protective Ottomans. They looked to Java, an island in the Indonesian archipelago in the Indian Ocean. The climate there was tropical and it had cool, volcanic mountains. The Portuguese had once tried to colonise this island, but they had withdrawn, leaving the Dutch to move into their trading stations.

Naturally, in Java there was no coffee culture. This was, of course, very unlike Yemen where, although cultivation of coffee was a commercial venture, it was also deeply embedded in the country's culture. This was the case, indeed, in much of the Middle East. Java's attitude to coffee was totally different. The people cultivating it worked under conditions of forced labour and they had no cultural investment in the crop they were growing and harvesting. Of course, in such conditions, it was unlikely that the coffee that was grown in Java was going to possess the quality of that produced in Yemen by farmers whose knowledge had been passed down to them by generations of their ancestors.

True though that may be, it must also be noted that for many people drinking coffee in Europe, they had nothing to which they could compare the beans produced in Java. They were mostly new to the drink and were happy to consume what was put in front of them. There was also the fact the coffee that had been served in coffee shops was very often not made from the best or freshest coffee beans. Indeed, the beans used in coffee shops were often old and mildewed. Cheap sugar made even the worst coffee drinkable and enabled consumers to obtain their required stimulus from the drink, no matter the quality of the beans. And, anyway, no one was the slightest bit aware that the coffee beans being used were not from the usual sources. It was a matter of little relevance to them.

The coffee beans produced in Java may initially have been a little dubious, but as time went on, it became evident that the conditions and the volcanic soil in the foothills of the island were ideal for the cultivation of the coffee bush. This was a huge investment of time, money and people by the Dutch. There were all the years to wait before the plant could be propagated and then there was a four-year wait before the first crop of beans could be harvested. Lack of experience also provided problems. No one had experience of growing coffee; they had to learn on the job.

Personnel was a problem. Plantations in the Caribbean were worked by slaves, but there was no such workforce on Java. Therefore, the Dutch brought in thousands of Chinese workers as well as natives from other parts of the Indonesian archipelago, who worked under a form of contract labour. There had, of course, already been lucrative crops in the area – crops for the spice trade – that provided a model for growing coffee. The inhabitants of the Banda islands, for instance, had successfully cultivated nutmeg and many of them were transported by force 1,000 miles to Java to work in the coffee plantations. Not many survived.

In 1718, the Dutch brought coffee cultivation to Surinam. Three years previously, it had been introduced to Haiti and

Santo Domingo. These plants were later supplemented by the hardier variety from Martinique. In the 1720s, plants from French Guiana were used to launch Brazil's first coffee plantation at Pará in the north of the country although it failed. In 1730, the British brought coffee to Jamaica and it was introduced into the Philippines in 1740. Don José Antonio Gelabert brought coffee to Cuba and ten years later the Dutch were extending coffee cultivation into the island of Celebes (now Sulawesi), east of Borneo. At the same time, it was arriving in Guatemala and was tried once more by the Portuguese in their colonies of Pará and Amazonias in Brazil. Brazil possessed the soil and climate that coffee propagation required and soon it was thriving in the areas of Rio, Minás, Espirito Santo and São Paulo. It was brought to Costa Rica from Cuba in 1779 and Venezuela in 1784.

The British government, driven by the popularity of coffee and the increasing demand for it, decided to promote interest in cultivating it in its colonial possessions. The first place it was tried was Jamaica where cultivation began in 1730. After a couple of years, it proved to be very promising, leading to a government reduction of import duty on coffee originating in the colonies from two shillings to one shilling and sixpence a pound. The British were a little late to the party as the French had already started cultivating coffee beans at Martinique, Hispaniola and on the Isle de Bourbon, near Madagascar, while the Dutch were growing coffee bushes in Surinam. So far, however, none of the coffee produced was a match for what was grown in Arabia.

Meanwhile, the British East India Company, which had lost out to the French and the Dutch in the race to make money from coffee, was putting all of its efforts into cultivating tea. Between 1700 and 1710 around 800,000 pounds of tea were imported into Britain. By 1721, this had risen to over a million pounds and the figure was 4 million by 1757. It had remained expensive and was not widely drunk, as a result. Therefore, the British government removed the tax on it, and by 1785, smuggling, which had made it affordable to the general public, was eliminated. Tea – not coffee – had become the national drink of the English.

'...coffee houses have been universally deemed the most convenient places of resort, because at a small expense of time or money, persons wanted may be found and spoke with, appointments made, current news heard, and whatever it most concerns us to know.'

'A Friend to the City', *The New York Journal*,
9 October 1775

4

Merchants, Revolutionaries and Bankers

Coffee Arrives in North America

It was Captain John Smith, founder of the Colony of Virginia at Jamestown in 1607, who was responsible for the introduction of coffee into North America. Smith was an extraordinary individual, a soldier and an adventurer who had served as a mercenary in the army of the French King Henry IV (r. 1589-1610), fighting for Dutch independence against King Philip II of Spain (r. 1556-98). He next turned up in the Mediterranean where he was involved in trade and piracy. Later, he fought against the Ottoman Empire in the war known as the Long Turkish War or the Thirteen Years' War, waged between the Habsburg Empire and the Ottomans, and was knighted by the Prince of Transylvania, Sigismund Báthory (r. 1586-98), for extraordinary courage in battle. He was captured by Crimean Tatars and sold as a slave but, after his Greek mistress fell in love with him and took him to the Crimea, he escaped. By 1604, he was back in England. Sometime during these extraordinary adventures Smith became familiar with coffee.

The Dutch West India Company established a settlement on Manhattan Island in 1624, but despite their consumption of coffee back home, they did not take any coffee beans with them to North America. Instead, they appear to have taken tea to their New Amsterdam settlement prior to bringing supplies of coffee. Similarly, when the *Mayflower* sailed from Plymouth to the New World in 1620, carrying 102 Pilgrims, there was no record in the ship's manifest of coffee, although there was a mortar and pestle on board, later used to make 'coffee powder'. By 1668, a drink, made from roasted beans and flavoured with honey, sugar or cinnamon, was being made in New York, as the New Amsterdam settlement had been renamed after the English had taken it over from the Dutch. In 1670, there was a reference to coffee in the official records of the New England colony and, 13 years later, William Penn (1644-1718) is known to have been purchasing coffee beans at the market in New York for his Pennsylvania colony. Soon coffee houses, modelled on the English and continental version, were established in places such as Norfolk, Virginia, St Louis and New Orleans.

Boston

Coffee had been known and drunk in London for 18 years before it came to Boston. The city's first coffee house was opened in 1670, established to serve the needs of Boston merchants in the Massachusetts Bay Colony. At that time, Boston was the largest city in North America, home to 7,000 citizens. It enjoyed close ties with British cities on the other side of the Atlantic, not least because it was the commercial centre of the American colonies which meant that there was close contact between its merchants and their British associates. Boston merchants will have encountered London coffee culture on their trips to England and they desired the same for their home city, places where they could meet and do business. British officials and businessmen, travelling back and forward to the colonies, would also be in need of the sustenance that could be found in the coffee house. Licences had traditionally been issued every year to what were termed 'houses of publique entertainment' – generally taverns and eating houses – but on 30 November 1670, the council granted the right to two women – 'Mrs Dorothy Jones the wife of Mr Morgan Jones' was 'approved to keepe a house of publique Entertainment for the sellinge of Coffee & Chuculettoe.' 'Jane the wife of Bartholomew Barnard' was similarly approved 'to keepe a house of publique entertainment for the sellinge of Coffee & chuculettoe.'

Licences for these first coffee houses were reviewed annually until 1674 and then in 1676, the council was persuaded by some 'Merchants & Gentlemen' to licence another coffee house. The owner of that establishment was one John Sparrow and it was perfectly situated, next to the Exchange and surrounded by bookshops. It was Sparrow's aim to make it Boston's principal meeting place for merchants. In 1690, the bookseller Benjamin Harris gained a licence for a coffee shop close to the Town House on King Street. Harris had emigrated to New England in 1686, leaving behind the bookshop he had owned in London. Apparently, the Protestant content of many of the publications he offered for sale came to the attention of James II's licensing authorities, forcing him to flee the country. In his London Coffee House in Boston, he sold books, pamphlets and almanacs imported from London and he even began publishing the North American colonies' first monthly newspaper, *Publick Occurrences*. Naturally, this was frowned upon by the authorities and was suppressed as soon as it first appeared, ostensibly because it was unlicensed. Harris sailed back to London in 1695, by which time the Gutteridge Coffee-house had opened for business. Robert Gutteridge was the brother-in-law of the printer, Nicholas Buttolph, publisher of the influential theologian and scientist, Cotton Mather (1663-1728), remembered today for his involvement in the Salem witch trials. Gutteridge ran his coffee house in a room in Buttolph's bookshop until the building was destroyed by fire in 1711. Nonetheless, by that time, coffee houses were thriving in Boston, and from the 1670s, they had provided Bostonians with a satisfactory simulacrum of the establishments that were such an important part of London's cultural and commercial life.

Coffee house taverns also sprang up, amongst them, the Indian Queen which operated for about 145 years before changing its name to the Washington Coffee House. It became the starting point for the Roxbury 'hourlies', stage coaches that ran every hour from Boston to Roxbury, five miles away.

The Sun Tavern opened its doors in 1690 and remained open until 1902 when it was demolished to make way for a skyscraper. The most famous of the Boston taverns, however, was the Green Dragon on Union Street, in the city's business centre. It remained in business from 1697 until 1832 and played a significant part in many of the major events of American history. Described by the American statesman Daniel Webster (1782-1852) as the 'headquarters of the Revolution', it hosted British redcoats, colonial governors, crown officers, British nobility, members of the political elite, revolutionaries, Boston Tea Party conspirators and Revolutionary generals. Revolutionaries Joseph Warren (1741-75), future President John Adams (1735-1826), James Otis Jr (1725-83) and Paul Revere (1734-1818) regularly met there. Meanwhile, the British coffee house was the venue for loyalists to the Crown and sometimes the antipathy the clientele of each felt for the other would spill over into physical attacks. James Otis, for instance, was so badly beaten in the British coffee house that he never regained his formerly impressive skills as an orator. The Bunch of Grapes was another hotbed of revolutionary thought. In 1776, it was almost destroyed when a delegate from the Second Continental Congress in Philadelphia read the Declaration of Independence from its balcony to a crowd assembled below.

The zenith of the Boston coffee house arrived in 1808 with the opening, after three years of construction work, of the Exchange coffee house. Designed by Charles Bulfinch (1763-1844), the most eminent architect of his day, it was possibly the most ambitious coffee house project ever, standing seven storeys high and costing half a million dollars. The Exchange resembled Lloyd's of London in that it became the centre of marine intelligence in the city. Every day it was crammed with mariners, naval officers and maritime insurance brokers. The first floor of the building was devoted to trading while the next floor was taken up by a large dining room in which banquets were staged, including one in honour of President James Monroe (1758-1831) in July 1817 that was attended by former President John Adams and a plethora of generals, senior naval officers and leading lights of the legal profession. On the floors above, there were more than 200 bedrooms. After the Exchange was destroyed by fire in 1818, another coffee house bearing that name was built on its site, but it bore little resemblance to the grand establishment that had previously stood there.

New York

The importance of the coffee house to New Yorkers as a public meeting place, can be seen in a letter, written by 'A Friend to the City' in *The New York Journal* of 9 October 1775:

...coffee houses have been universally deemed the most convenient places of resort, because at a small expense of time or money, persons wanted may be found and spoke with, appointments made, current news heard, and whatever it most concerns us to know. In all cities, therefore, and large towns that I have seen in the British dominions, sufficient encouragement has been given to support one or more coffee houses in a genteel manner. How comes it then that New York, the most central, and one of the largest and most prosperous cities in British America, cannot support one coffee house? It is a scandal to the city and its inhabitants to be destitute of such a convenience for want of due encouragement. A coffee house, indeed, there is, a very good and comfortable one, extremely well-tended and accommodated, but it is frequented but by an inconsiderable number of people; And I have observed with surprise, that but a small part of those who do frequent it, contribute anything at all to the expense of it, but come in and go out without calling for or paying anything to the house. In all the coffee houses of London, it is customary for every one that comes in to call for at least a dish of coffee, or leave the value of one, which is but reasonable, because when the keepers of these houses have been at the expense of setting them up and providing all necessaries for the accommodation of company, every one that comes to receive the benefit of these conveniences ought to contribute something towards the expense of them.

Coffee began to replace 'must' or beer at breakfast in New York and it was not long before coffee houses, somewhat on the London model, began to open. As elsewhere, they quickly became centres of business and politics as well as a vital part of the social life of New Yorkers. In the beginning, however, they were never the literary hothouses that many European coffee houses were, since professional writers were in short supply in the city at the time. Unusually, however, they took on even greater importance in New York as their long rooms were sometimes used as courthouses as well as for the general assembly meetings of the colonists or even for council meetings. The British-style coffee shop was also an attempt by Governor Benjamin Fletcher (1640-1703) to anglicise the city after four decades of Dutch rule and to counter the influence of the rebellious Calvinist settlers who were descended from Dutch settlers.

It is often said that the first coffee house in North America was opened in New York. The earliest record in support of this shows that on 1 November 1696, John Hutchins bought a piece of land on Broadway on which he built a coffee house at the sign of the King's Arms. It was located just north of Trinity Church, the first Anglican church to be built in the colony. Its location is close to where the World Trade Centre stood. (Some sources suggest, however, that Boston's London Coffee House poured its first coffee in 1689, some years before Hutchins' establishment.) Even if it was not the first, the King's Arms was an interesting establishment, built on two storeys of wood and yellow brick brought from Holland. On the roof were seats which provided a wonderful view of the bay, the river and the city. The main room on the ground floor was lined with booths, separated by green curtains for privacy. On the first floor, meetings could be held and business conducted. It swiftly became the hub of English New York, patronised by municipal and provincial officials, merchants and officers from the garrison at the fort. At the King's Arms, men of the 'English party' met to discuss the latest news and argue about politics. Hutchins was no stranger to political debate. In 1702, he was in trouble with the authorities for collecting signatures for petitions that were critical of the authoritative style of the city's rulers.

Meeting rooms were common to coffee houses and unlikely to be found in a tavern. Another difference between a coffee house and a tavern was that men went to coffee houses in order to conduct business, while the customers of a tavern sought entertainment or lodgings. For many years the King's Arms remained New York's only coffee house and was consequently known simply as 'the coffee house' rather than the King's Arms.

Although its exact location is unknown, the New Coffee House was dispensing its wares in September 1709 when, according to the *Journal of the General Assembly of New York*, a conference was held there. Another, the Exchange Coffee House, was mentioned in a 1730 advertisement that announced a sale of land by public auction there. It is believed to have been situated at the end of Broad Street next to the sea wall. In those days this area was the business centre of New York and the Exchange was the only coffee house in the city. By the end of the decade, it was an auction house as well as a place to drink coffee. By 1750, however, it

137

had lost some of its lustre and its name was changed to the Gentleman's Exchange coffee house and tavern. A year later it moved to Broadway and lost the word 'Exchange' from its title. In 1753, it moved to Hunter's Quay, now named Front Street between the current Old Slip and Wall Street. Soon, though, it was no more, replaced in New Yorkers' affections by the Merchants' coffee house. This was opened, on an unknown date, by Daniel Bloom, a sailor who had purchased the Jamaica Pilot Boat Tavern in 1737. It was situated on the northwest corner of modern-day Wall Street and Water Street. Bloom ran it until his death around 1750 when it was taken over first by Captain James Ackland and then, not long after, by Luke Roome. The building was sold in 1758 but leased to Mary Ferrari who later moved the Merchants' coffee house across the road to the southeast corner of Water Street and Wall Street. She remained in charge until May 1776, when it was taken over by Cornelius Bradford, although by that time it was losing its clientele. Bradford fled when the British took over New York during the Revolution and the Merchants' became a place where the ships they captured were sold. In 1779, the Chamber of Commerce resumed its sessions in the long room upstairs, after it had been suspended during the war and the occupation. In 1781, the Queen's Head Tavern proprietor, John Strachan, took over. He advertised his establishment, stating that he aimed to:

...pay attention not only as a Coffee House, but as a tavern, in the truest; and to distinguish the same as the

City Tavern and Coffee House, with constant and best attendance. Breakfast from seven to eleven; soups and relishes from eleven to half-past one. Tea, coffee, etc., in the afternoon, as in England.

After peace came in 1783, Bradford returned, assuming control once more of the Merchants', and announcing that in his establishment, 'Interesting intelligence will be carefully collected and the greatest attention will be given to the arrival of vessels, when trade and navigation shall resume their former channels'. His coffee house became a hub for shipping news and also kept a directory of returning New Yorkers, 'where any gentleman now resident in the city may insert their names and place of residence', an early instance of a city directory. Bradford was an energetic marketer and had soon restored the Merchants' to the heart of the New York business community. Naturally, when he died in 1786, his funeral was held in the coffee house to which he had devoted so much of his life.

The Merchants' eventually burned down in 1804 but, during its existence, it had been host to many tumultuous events: the reading of the warning to citizens to stop rioting against the 1765 Stamp Act; debates about the refusal to import goods from Great Britain; the demonstrations by the Sons of Liberty against the landing of his cargo of tea by Captain Lockyer of the *Nancy* which had been barred entry to Boston Harbour in 1774; a general meeting of citizens in May of that year about the relationship with the Massachusetts colony that produced a letter calling for a congress of representatives from the colonies and suggesting a 'virtuous and spirited Union' and mass gatherings in 1775 following the Battles of Lexington and Concord, the first military engagements of the American Civil War. It was also the venue for meetings of various large groups, ending with the Committee of One Hundred, around the time of the American Revolutionary War, 'in order to consult on measures proper to be pursued on the present critical and important situation'. In effect, the Merchants' coffee house became the seat of government for the colonies. During the war, on 23 April 1789, George Washington, recently elected the first president of the United States, was officially welcomed at the coffee house by the governor of the state as well as other state and city officials. Here, in 1784, the Bank of New York, the city's first financial institution, was created and, six years later, the first sale of stocks by sworn brokers took place there.

After the fiery demise of the Merchants' coffee house in 1804, the most famous coffee house in New York was the Tontine which had been created by 157 New York merchants in 1791 who had wanted a larger coffee house establishment in which to conduct their business. Each of them had shares in the establishment and, when one died, his shares reverted to the other shareholders rather than to his heirs. It was named Tontine in recognition of a similar scheme – a form of life insurance – introduced in France in 1653 by the Italian banker Lorenzo Tonti (c. 1602-84). The investors bought the building on the northwest corner of Wall Street and Water Street, where the original Merchants' coffee house had stood and also purchased the adjoining lots. It opened with a grand banquet on 5 June 1792, hosted by the establishment's first landlord, John Hyde, and was described by an English visitor to the city in 1794:

The Tontine tavern and coffee house is a handsome large brick building; you ascend six or eight steps under a portico, into a large public room, which is the Stock Exchange of New York, where all bargains are made. Here are two books kept, as at Lloyd's [in London] of every ship's arrival and clearance. This house was built for the accommodation of the merchants by Tontine shares of two hundred pounds each. It is kept by Mr Hyde, formerly a woollen draper in London. You can lodge and board there at a common table, and you pay ten shillings currency a day, whether you dine out or not.

In 1817, the stock market based itself at the Tontine and named itself the New York Stock and Exchange Board. It remained there until 1827 when it moved to the Merchants' Exchange Building. It continued as a coffee house until 1834 when it was let as business space, after competition from the Merchants' Exchange coffee house had proved too strong. About 1850, a new five-storey building was erected on the site, costing around $60,000, which is said to have been the first real office building in New York. Today, the site is occupied by a large office block which has retained the name Tontine. It was owned until 1920 by coffee merchants John B and Charles A O'Donahue when it was bought for a million dollars by the Federal Sugar Refining Company.

The great era of the New York coffee house had ended long before, as restaurants and hotels opened to cater for the beverage needs of customers, and clubs assumed the social function of establishments such as the Merchants' and the Tontine.

Philadelphia

As has been noted, William Penn brought coffee to the Quaker colony that he had founded in 1682. Initially, coffee was too expensive, a cup costing around 17 cents, when a meal was just 12. Tea was, therefore, a far more popular beverage, but the Stamp Act and the tax on tea of 1767 led to a tea boycott which the Pennsylvania colony joined. Coffee benefited from this action, soon becoming by far the beverage most frequently drunk in the colonies that would form the original 13 states. The coffee houses that sprang up played an important part in the history of the city of Philadelphia and in that of the United States. The most important of these were Ye Coffee House, two with the same name of the London Coffee House, and the City Tavern that was also known as the Merchants' Coffee House. (This is not to be confused with the equally famous establishment of the same name in New York.) The coffee house was initially a meeting place in the city for Quaker municipal officials, mariners and merchants who transacted business there but the approach of the American Revolution brought colonists to the tables to vent their anger at what they saw as British oppression in the colonies. Once independence had been secured, the coffee house became a venue for social functions and eating.

Philadelphia's first coffee house was established around 1700 by Samuel Carpenter, on Front Street. Known as Ye Coffee House, for a number of years it remained the only such enterprise. It is not known how long it lasted but there is a mention of it being in the possession of a certain Henry Flower in 1703. Flower was the province's postmaster at the time and Ye Coffee House also served as a post office. An advert of 1734, placed in Benjamin Franklin's *Gazette*, implies that Ye Coffee House was still plying its trade then:

> All persons who are indebted to Henry Flower, late postmaster of Pennsylvania, for Postage of Letters or otherwise, are desir'd to pay the same to him at the old Coffee House in Philadelphia.

The second notable coffee establishment in Philadelphia was the London Coffee House. One version of this existed in 1702, but the location is disputed. It catered for the wealthier elements of society whereas Ye Coffee House was more suited to business types. The London Coffee House did, however, host the province's General Assembly in 1733. Roberts' Coffee House was situated in Front Street, probably opening around 1740. It was the venue for a public banquet to thank the captain of the British vessel *Otter* that rescued Philadelphia from an attack by French and Spanish privateers during the French and Indian War of 1754 to 1763.

The most famous coffee house in Philadelphia was established by William Bradford, the publisher of the *Pennsylvania Journal*. Located on the southwest corner of Second and Market Streets it was, like the earlier coffee house described above, named the London Coffee House. Bradford justified his intentions for the establishment to the Governor as follows:

Having been advised to keep a Coffee House for the benefit of merchants and traders, and as some people may at times be desirous to be furnished with other liquors besides coffee, your petitioner apprehends it is necessary to have the Governor's licence.

Like the Tontine, it seems to have been a venture in which a number of people had shares as Bradford invited subscribers to a meeting to discuss his plans. The London was a success, described as 'the pulsating heart of excitement, enterprise, and patriotism' of Philadelphia. It was frequented by influential people and businessmen. Travellers from other colonies and from abroad frequented it in order to meet the right people and the Governor himself was a customer along with other officials who went there 'to sip their coffee from the hissing urn'. Auctions of all manner of things, including horses, foodstuffs and carriages, were held there. Slaves – black men, women and children – were even auctioned there, exhibited beforehand on a platform built outside the establishment.

Bradford joined the Revolutionary army as a major and gave up running the coffee house. He would rise to the rank of colonel but, after independence had been achieved, he returned to the coffee business. By that time, however, there was too much competition and business suffered, forcing him to relinquish the lease in 1780.

Modelled on London's coffee houses, the City Tavern, built in 1773, and later known as the Merchants' coffee house, was one of Bradford's principal competitors. Three storeys in height, it had several large rooms that could be converted into a large dining room that was 50 feet long. Its first owner, Daniel Smith, had struggled against the nearby London Coffee House before the Revolution, but after independence, he began to overtake the London and for the next 25 years his establishment was the most popular meeting place in Philadelphia. The date when it changed its name to the Merchants' coffee house is not known, but it was certainly called that when its new proprietor, James Kitchen, took ownership at the start of the nineteenth century. In 1806, facing stiff competition from restaurants and hotels, he transformed it into a mercantile exchange.

'These were senates in miniature; here mighty political questions were discussed; here peace and war were decided upon; here generals were brought to the bar of justice... distinguished orators were victoriously refuted, ministers heckled upon their ignorance, their incapacity, their perfidy, their corruption. The café is in reality a French institution; in them we find all these agitations and movements of men, the like of which is unknown in the English tavern. No government can go against the sentiment of the cafés. The Revolution took place because they were for the Revolution. Napoleon reigned because they were for glory. The Restoration was shattered, because they understood the Charter in a different manner.'

Narcisse-Achille de Salvandy (1795-1856),
French politician

5

Coffee in the Eighteenth Century

Germany

In some places, as the eighteenth century began, coffee was no longer a novelty. Ports such as Venice in Italy and Marseille in France, had become used to the exotic new products that the seventeenth century had brought. As well as coffee, there were nutmeg, silks, pepper and other exotic spices. The Mediterranean was already very familiar with such novelties when they were first coming to the notice of the peoples of northern Europe. Indeed, although coffee was known, even inland, in places such as Germany, which did have ports and trade, the café and coffee house phenomenon was slow in arriving. In those turbulent times, coffee had been brought north by soldiers and, as we have seen, it was Ottoman soldiers who took coffee to the gates of Vienna. Germany's coffee had, in the seventeenth century, arrived from Ottoman sources, the supply chain bringing it via Italy and the southern French coast, principally the port of Marseille. This changed in the eighteenth century and Germany began importing its coffee mainly from the Caribbean. It arrived in Bordeaux, London or Amsterdam and was transported to Hamburg. Brokers in Bremen and Leipzig would then distribute it throughout the country. However, it would not be until the middle of the century, with supplies coming from the West Indies, that prices began to come down and coffee became more widely affordable.

Generally, in Europe, the development of café culture emerged from the sweeping social, political and economic changes that were taking place. In the Habsburg Empire and Germany, coffee had been consumed extensively before the rise of the middle class engendered a new and vibrant café culture. There were places that served coffee but which could not be described as coffee houses – on the streets, in public spaces and in people's homes. The phenomenon of *Kaffeekränzchen* – 'coffee circles' – rose in popularity in the late seventeenth and eighteenth centuries, enhancing the status of women in the country and even influencing the way houses were designed internally. No bourgeois, middle-class house was complete without a parlour in which coffee could be served. Meanwhile, the number of coffee houses in Germany grew only very slowly. There were six in Hamburg, for instance, in 1700 and that number had only risen to 20 a century later. The same can be said for many other German cities.

Great Britain

In Britain, on the other hand, there was a proliferation of coffee houses. It is difficult to say how many there were in London by the end of the seventeenth century but, according to one writer, by 1714 they were 'innumerable'. In his *Cyclopaedia* of 1727, the writer and encyclopaedist, Ephraim Chambers (c. 1680-1740), estimated the number of coffee houses in London to be 3,000, although some sources claim this to be a gross exaggeration and that the number was closer to 500. For his *History of London* in 1739, the Scottish topographer and historian, William Maitland (c. 1693-1757), spent 11 months walking throughout London, recording the names of the streets, the public buildings, the number of houses, breweries, public houses and coffee houses on each street. This incredibly industrious man counted 551 coffee houses. At the time, the inhabitants of the capital numbered just around half a million which meant that they were more than adequately supplied with establishments where they could while away the hours for a penny and the price of a cup of coffee. It is interesting to note, however, that these establishments were not spread evenly across the city. Rather, they were mainly situated in the wealthier areas, in particular the City, St James's and around Covent Garden and Fleet Street. There were far fewer in the areas of London where poorer people lived. In fact, the establishments that were present in large numbers were not coffee houses or even taverns; they were the brandy houses selling brandy and gin. Maitland counted no fewer than 8,000 of those.

Coffee houses continued in their role as meeting places for businessmen as well as places of relaxation. 'These coffee houses,' one European visitor remarked, 'are the constant rendezvous for men of business as well as the idle people so that a man is sooner asked about his coffee house than his lodgings.' He was far from complimentary about their ambience: '...in other respects they are loathsome, full of smoke, like a guard room and as much crowded. I believe 'tis these places that furnish the inhabitants with slander for there one hears exact accounts of everything done in town as if it were but a village'.

They were not all bad, however. A typical establishment of the time would possess a certain homeliness. There would be a roaring fire and large cast-iron pots of water would be constantly boiling away. The furnishings consisted normally of long wooden tables and stools. Behind the counter would stand a woman who guarded the payment kiosk, accepting the entry coin of one penny. She would also take the two pennies required to purchase a cup of coffee.

Coffee houses in England were classified according to the type of custom they attracted. Naturally, in the City of London, it was often wealthy merchants who frequented them, doing deals away from the Exchange, probably more quickly and certainly more privately. Others went to specific coffee houses in order to meet certain types of people. Someone interested in literature would pay his penny entry fee at a coffee house that writers were known to frequent. In an historical painting of 1858 by the nineteenth century artist, Eyre Crowe (1824-1910), for instance, the poet, Alexander Pope, is seen meeting his fellow poet, John Dryden (1631-1700) at Will's coffee house. The painting features portraits of some of the greatest literary minds who were former or current customers of this particular establishment. Amongst them are Richard Steele (1672-1729), John Vanbrugh (1664-1726), Joseph Addison (1672-1719) and Thomas Southerne (1660-1746).

Business, however, was still central to the eighteenth-century coffee house in England. Men who had unfortunately been declared bankrupt would meet their creditors in coffee houses. Perhaps the neutral ground and the fact that other people were present brought calm to the no doubt fraught discussions. Auctions were held there, an example being the book and copyright auctions that were held at Sheffield's coffee house in 1700. Indeed, the book and newspaper trades developed a useful association with coffee houses. As ever, certain establishments specialised in publishers, authors or journalists. In contrast to their equivalents on the continent, though, these were far from what could be described as literary salons. Rather, the English counterpart was more of a competitive debating society. English novelist and historian, Walter Besant (1836-1901), described it:

The coffee-houses were great schools of conversation. A man had to hold his own against a whole roomful of men eager to show their wit. The custom encouraged readiness and clearness of expression and of thought. Younger men did not venture to speak in some coffee-houses. And it is not sufficiently understood, in reading

Johnson's sententious phrases, that his words were often spoken in a coffee-house so as to be heard by the whole listening room. So Dryden delivered his judgments, and was admired and worshipped by the younger men, as the oracle of the coffee-house. They, indeed, sat mute, diffident, afraid to speak in so great a presence; or, if they hazarded an opinion, did so with the greatest diffidence, and congratulated themselves afterwards if it had been favourably received.

Thus, the coffee house in the eighteenth century was a hub for news, for arranging meetings with people, a commercial market-place for businessmen and merchants, and a place where the dandy could parade, and the wit could demonstrate the heights of his intelligence. It was, according to John Ashton (1834-1911), the nineteenth century social historian, writing from the middle-class perspective of his own time, a great social leveller – 'a neutral meeting-ground for all men'. At the same time, however, he pointed out that men still assorted in coffee houses with others of the same calibre. Ashton also noted that bad language was punished by a fine of one shilling and if someone started an argument, he had to buy everyone a coffee. Card-playing or gambling with dice were banned in coffee houses and, if a wager was made, it was not permitted to exceed the amount of five shillings. Discussion of religion was also not allowed.

Newspapers were very important in the development of the coffee house, even as their popularity began to wane during the eighteenth century and the middle and upper echelons of society began to swap their allegiance to the private club. As newspapers became more available in coffee houses, they became places where men lower on the perceived social ladder came to read rather than do business or debate the great issues of the day. They could not afford a daily newspaper but they could read it at the coffee house which would usually have three or four available for free. Smaller tradesmen and craftsmen and the clerk, therefore, began to frequent coffee houses to read about politics and scandals, rather than debate about them, as had once been the case. Conversation ceased to be the currency of the coffee shop and it began to be cloaked in a library-like, reverential silence.

The Eighteenth Century Coffee House as Stock Exchange

In the 1690s, the coffee houses had started to introduce specialist news for their particular type of customer. Garraway's, for instance, provided a list of 'what Prices the Actions bear of most Companies trading in Joynt-Stocks'. They also maintained a library of books that listed commodity prices, rates of foreign exchange and the prices of government stocks. Newspapers also printed commodity prices. Some publications specialised in overseas trade, providing lists of imported goods. A marine list offered the movements of shipping, arriving and departing at British ports as well as at foreign ones. As we have seen, Edward Lloyd began publishing his marine list in 1692.

The coffee house also became incredibly important to the financial markets. Prices on the market could be altered by a chance encounter and conversation over a cup of coffee. The very structure of the stock exchange emerged from the coffee house. Auctions were often held and allowed the sale and purchase of securities, but it was at best a limited solution. Another method was to create the role of the broker, an operative who had the job of finding buyers or sellers for people who wished to buy or sell securities. By the start of the eighteenth century, these stockbrokers were working away in coffee houses. Jobbers also came into being – individuals who bought and sold stocks for themselves and who also ensured that buyers and sellers were brought together. Exchange Alley was the hub for jobbers, as explained by Daniel Defoe in 1719 in his pamphlet *The Anatomy of Exchange Alley: or, A System of Stock-Jobbing*:

The Center of the Jobbing is in the Kingdom of Exchange-Alley, and its Adjacencies; the Limits, are easily surrounded in about a Minute and a half (viz.) stepping out of Jonathan's into the Alley, you turn your Face full South, moving on a few Paces, and then turning Due East, you advance to Garraway's; from thence going out at the other Door, you go on still East into Birchin-Lane, and then halting a little at the Sword-Blade Bank to do much Mischief in fewest Words, you immediately face to the North, enter Cornhill, visit two or three petty

Provinces there in your way West: And thus having Box'd your Compass, and sail'd round the whole Stock-Jobbing Globe, you turn into Jonathan's again; and so, as most of the great Follies of Life oblige us to do, you end just where you began.

Indeed, the stocks and commodity exchanges of the current time – even where the trading floor has become electronic – owe a good deal to the system developed in eighteenth century London coffee houses. In the 'structured anarchy', as one observer calls it, of the trading floor, conduct is governed by group pressure and intimidation, as in the days of coffee house trading.

Jonathan's Coffee House was situated in Exchange Alley. It had been opened around 1680 by Jonathan Miles and, in 1698, a broker named John Castaing began posting the current prices of stocks and commodities there. That same year, a number of dealers who had been expelled from the Royal Exchange for bad behaviour, took their business to Jonathan's. Jonathan's was the venue for important moments in the history of share-dealing, including the notorious South Sea Bubble that ruined thousands of investors, and the panic of 1745 when Jacobite forces reached Derby and caused a run on the banks in London. By 1761, stockbrokers resented sharing space at Jonathan's with ordinary customers who had popped into the coffee house to drink coffee and read the newspaper. Or they could even turn themselves into brokers for the day, all for just 6 pence for which they would receive pen, ink and paper and a small cup of coffee or chocolate. Therefore, 150 brokers came to an agreement with the proprietor of Jonathan's that would grant them exclusive use of the establishment for three hours a day for £1,200 a year. During those three hours, the coffee shop would be available only to members who paid an annual fee of £8. One of the coffee house's customers objected to this exclusivity and took the case to court where Lord Mansfield (1705-93) ruled that the exclusivity they sought was incompatible with the normal business of a coffee house. As he noted, 'Jonathan's had been a market (time out of mind) for buying and selling government securities'. Disappointed, the brokers had no option but to abandon Jonathan's and establish their own place of business. In 1771, they obtained the lease on a piece of land in Sweeting's Alley, close to Threadneedle Street, and they moved into their newly constructed building in 1773. To begin with, it was known as New Jonathan's but the name was soon changed to the Stock Exchange. Meanwhile, back at old Jonathan's, its most lucrative custom having decamped, business went downhill. This was also bad news for the area which relied on the traders coming and going from the coffee house.

France

Café Procope was one of the earliest in Paris, but it set the tone for the café in the French capital with its large, high-ceilinged rooms and ornate stylings. Its crystal chandeliers, elegant tapestries, mirrored ceilings, gilded features and sumptuous velvet curtains were copied in countless other establishments. They were usually situated adjacent to busy markets where custom from stall-holders and customers was virtually guaranteed. The furnishings and ambience were very different to the English version with its long wooden tables and stools. The typical Parisian café looked very much like it does today – small, circular marble-topped tables surrounded by elegant little chairs. Many added alcoholic drinks to their offering as well as food.

Unlike their English equivalents, which became less political, Parisian cafés became increasingly so as the eighteenth century progressed. The French Revolution of 1789 was foreshadowed in the heated discussions which took place within their walls. Like London cafés at the time of Charles II, they became the haunts of royalists and republicans, each side taking up residence in its own particular places and within them debate raged and intrigue hung menacingly in the atmosphere.

The monarchy and its agents kept a close eye on Café Procope, even after Louis XV's death from smallpox. As we have seen, it was frequented by a number of the men who would lead the French to revolution, including Robespierre, Marat, Danton and Desmoulins. The coffee houses of the Palais Royal also became home to revolutionaries and the air would crackle with condemnations of King Louis XVI (r. 1774-92). One visitor to Paris at the time describes the scenes in the coffee houses of the era:

The coffee houses present yet more singular and astounding spectacles; they are not only crowded within, but other expectant crowds are at the doors and windows, listening à gorge déployée to certain orators who from chairs or tables harangue each his little audience; the eagerness with which they are heard, and the thunder of applause they receive for every sentiment of more than common hardiness or violence against the government, cannot easily be imagined.

The role cafés played in the French Revolution cannot be overestimated. French politician, Narcisse-Achille de Salvandy (1795-1856), wrote:

These were senates in miniature; here mighty political questions were discussed; here peace and war were decided upon; here generals were brought to the bar of justice... distinguished orators were victoriously refuted, ministers heckled upon their ignorance, their incapacity, their perfidy, their corruption. The café is in reality a French institution; in them we find all these agitations and movements of men, the like of which is unknown in the English tavern. No government can go against the sentiment of the cafés. The Revolution took place because they were for the Revolution. Napoleon reigned because they were for glory. The Restoration was shattered, because they understood the Charter in a different manner.

The coffee houses at the Palais Royal were hotbeds of debate before, during and after the French Revolution. In the frenetic month of July 1789, they were crowded and still more people pressed up against the windows and crowded the doorways, listening to speakers who argued furiously across the tables. Applause and approbation would ring out every time someone made a point against the government.

On Sunday 12 July the Palais area was teeming with people and the air crackled with tension. At the Café Foy, a young journalist, Camille Desmoulins (1760-94) jumped up on an outside table and began to deliver a vehemently anti-government speech, the first overt act of the French Revolution. At the conclusion of his speech, he had fired up his audience so much that they marched off with him to foment revolt. Two days later, the Bastille fell.

Interestingly, as if embarrassed by its involvement in such radical goings-on, the Café Foy would later become a sedate rendezvous for artists and writers. Until it closed, it was noted for its exclusivity and for its strictly administered 'no smoking' policy.

It has been said that around the turn of the eighteenth century, Paris became one vast café. One source describes what he termed the 'three ages of coffee'. The first was the time of Arabian coffee which was around during the decades before and after 1700, and was drunk from tiny cups by beautiful ladies in fashionable salons. Indian coffee arrived between 1710 and 1720, roughly during the period of the Régence (1715-23) when Philippe, Duke of Orléans (1674-1723) ruled as prince regent on behalf of the young King Louis XV. The coffee was from the island of Bourbon (now Réunion) which had been settled by the French in the sixteenth century. Coffee was planted in its volcanic soils. But it was insufficient for French needs and the French turned, as we have seen, to planting coffee bushes in the West Indies, heralding the third age. The historian, Michelet, described how:

The strong coffee of Santo Domingo, full, coarse, nourishing as well as stimulating, sustained the adult population of that period, the strong age of the encyclopedia. It was drunk by Buffon, Diderot, Rousseau, added its glow to glowing souls, its light to the penetrating vision of the prophets gathered in the cave of Procope, who saw at the bottom of the black beverage the future rays of '89. Danton, the terrible Danton, took several cups of coffee before mounting the tribune. 'The horse must have its oats,' he said.

Women and Café and Coffee House Culture

Cafés and coffee houses undoubtedly made a major contribution to creating a socially, politically and ethnically inclusive space, somewhere that, if you had the one penny entrance fee in England or, in Europe, the price of a coffee, you could enter at will and happily spend a day conversing, debating, catching up with the news or just watching the world go by. But only if you were male. Such establishments were strictly off-limits for women. Their coffee experiences were more likely to take place in domestic salons, sharing an afternoon with other women, although high-born ladies would often order their carriages to stop in front of cafés so that they could have coffee served to them in silver cups with saucers by a porter. And, of course, it was not like the Muslim world, where the behaviour of women was codified by holy law. It was the cultural mores of the day that kept women out of cafés and coffee houses.

That was not to say that women could not be used to attract custom. Indeed, it had long been recognised that sex appeal was a powerful marketing tool for coffee shops. It was well known and had been reported by European travellers that Ottoman coffee houses often hired attractive boys as waiters. The Portuguese Jewish merchant, Pedro Teixeira was of the opinion that the popularity of the coffee house with Turkish men was not solely due to coffee. He wrote of the 'pretty boys, richly dressed, who serve coffee and take the money...' suggesting that it was sex that brought men in. Poet Sir George Sandys (1577-1644) told how he witnessed 'many of the Coffa-men keeping beautifull boyes, who serve as stales to procure customers'. 'Stale' is a hunting metaphor, a 'stale' being a decoy bird that was used in London to describe the lowest class of prostitute. A 'stale' would lure a client into a place where he could be robbed by her associates. George Mainwaring, another member of Sir Anthony Shirley's expedition, wrote:

The owners of these houses do keep young boys: in some houses they have a dozen, some more, some less; they keep them very gallant in apparel; these boys are called Bardashes, which they do use in their beastly manner, instead of women, for all the summer time they keep their women very close in the houses, and have use of boys.

It is worth noting, by the way, that such accusations by Protestants were commonly used as attacks on Islam.

So, just as these establishments hired attractive boys to attract customers, sex was also used in French and English cafés in the eighteenth century. A pretty woman behind the counter was one more reason to visit the coffee house or café or to choose one over another. Sometimes, indeed, the attractiveness of the server determined the quality of a place rather than the coffee on offer. They were turbulent times, however, especially in France and change was in the air, social as well as political. Women were occasionally to be found amongst the artists and writers to be found in cafés. The only problem was that, in order to gain entry to these male bastions, they had to dress as men. The brilliant French natural philosopher and mathematician, Émilie du Châtelet (1706-49), tried to enter Café Gradot in Paris one day in 1734. This café was a well-known haunt of mathematicians, astronomers and scientists, and Pierre Louis Maupertuis (1698-1759) and other eminent mathematicians passed hours in the café locked in intense debate. When du Châtelet attempted to gain entry in order to listen to these great men and perhaps contribute to the discussion, she was prevented on account of her gender. Émilie du Châtelet was a very determined woman, however, and a week later, she was once more at the door of the café seeking entry, this time dressed as a man. In fact, she never believed that she would fool people into thinking she actually was a man but she wanted to emphasise how ridiculous the prohibition of women really was. The management relented and she was allowed into Café Gradot and, indeed, became a regular. Apparently the great Maupertuis found it all highly amusing.

The Boston Tea Party

As we have seen, the North American colonists, as loyal British subjects, mirrored the liking for coffee that manifested itself in Britain. But towards the end of the eighteenth century, encouraged by the British East India Company, the British began to drink tea rather than coffee. King George III wanted to raise more tax and introduced the Stamp Act 1765 in the North American colonies. When outrage ensued from the colonists and the demand came for 'No taxation without representation', the British Parliament relented and repealed all the taxes involved in the Stamp Act, except the tax they had imposed on tea. New taxes were levied through the Townshend Acts of 1767 and more boycotts and protests followed. A non-importation agreement was reached and colonists made a statement by resolving not to drink British tea. Alternatives were found, from Holland and Labrador, for example. Meanwhile, British tea continued to be imported into Boston until pressure was applied by protesters for it to stop. Again Parliament eventually relented, repealing the Townshend taxes in 1770, but the duty on tea remained. It was retained by the Prime Minister, Lord North (1732-92) who, by keeping it, was making the point that Britain had the right to tax the Americans. The repeal of the Townshend Act persuaded the Americans to stop boycotting British imports. From 1771 to 1773, tea was imported into America once more, and the three pence per pound duty was paid. Boston remained the biggest smuggler of illicit tea and a great deal was also imported into New York and Philadelphia. With the tax in place, sales of British tea plummeted, while the East India Company continued to import tea into Britain. The result was a huge surplus that was not being bought. The Company, one of the most important British commercial institutions, was in severe financial difficulty, the situation compounded by the dreadful famine that blighted Bengal between 1769 and 1773. It was determined that selling the tea cheaply in Europe would result in it being smuggled back into Britain where it would undercut the fully taxed product and deplete the government coffers. Reducing or eliminating the Townshend duty was not possible for the government who used the money received to pay the salaries of colonial officials such as governors and judges. Furthermore, North's government was determined to maintain the principle that it had the right to tax the colonies. The best market for the surplus tea, it was decided, was that of the American colonies.

The East India Company was given the right to export

tea to the colonies directly, eliminating middlemen. The Tea Act 1773 gave authority for 5,000 cases of tea to be shipped to the colonies and although tax of £1,750 would be paid by the importers when the cargo was landed, this tea would still undercut the smugglers and colonial tea importers. The Company realised the delicate nature of the tax and unsuccessfully tried to have it paid covertly.

When the tea ships arrived in Boston Harbour, 5,000 out of a population of 16,000 awaited them. Some dressed as Mohawk Indians and disguised their faces because of the illegal nature of their protest. Between 30 and 130 men boarded the ships and dumped every one of the 342 chests of tea overboard. The significance of this action cannot be overstated. As a result, Parliament responded in 1774 with the Intolerable Acts that, amongst other things, put an end to self-government in Massachusetts and established a blockade to prevent the use of the port of Boston for commerce. This brought more protest in the Thirteen Colonies and led to the convening of the First Continental Congress which called for the repeal of the Acts and organised resistance to them. The crisis eventually led to the outbreak of the American Revolutionary War in Boston in 1775, the overthrow of British rule and American independence.

One side effect was that across the colonies it become almost a patriotic duty to abstain from drinking tea. As future Founding Father and second president of the United States, John Adams wrote to his wife in 1774: 'Tea must be universally renounced, and I must be weaned, and the sooner the better.' The consumption of coffee in the colonies rose from 0.19 pounds per person in 1772 to 1.41 pounds in 1799. The fact that coffee was cheaper, because it did not have to be transported quite so far as tea, also helped increase its popularity. It would increasingly be coffee from their own hemisphere that Americans would import and drink.

Coffee and Slavery

The European colonial powers continued to take coffee plants to their colonies to spread its propagation. Of course, the labour used in this work was that of slaves, imported from Africa and making the perilous crossing of the Atlantic for that purpose.

The initial impetus for bringing slaves to the Caribbean was the harvesting of sugarcane. Sugar has been produced in the Indian subcontinent since ancient times, spreading through the Khyber Pass to Afghanistan. It was first grown in China in the seventh century, by which time it had become a culinary staple and was used to make desserts. Brought back to Europe by the Crusaders after their campaigns in the Holy Land, it began to supplement the use of honey which had until then been the only sweetener available. In the fifteenth century, Venice became the European centre for refining and distributing sugar. After the European settlement of Madeira and the Canary Islands and the planting of sugarcane there, however, sugar became more readily available, although still very expensive.

It was taken to the New World by Christopher Columbus (1451-1506), and the first harvest was undertaken in Hispaniola (now Haiti and the Dominican Republic) in 1501. By the 1520s, sugar mills had been established in Cuba and Jamaica and sugarcane was being grown in Brazil, having been taken there by the Portuguese. It would, of course, play an important role in the popularisation of coffee. By the eighteenth century, Santo Domingo was the richest colony in the Caribbean and Europe was very dependent on it for its coffee. Sixty per cent of all coffee drunk in its coffee houses and at home came from the island. It also exported sugar and its exports of the two crops, coffee and sugar, amounted to more than all the other islands of the Caribbean combined.

But, as more coffee was grown in the Caribbean, plantation owners decided to follow the model of sugarcane and began to import slaves to carry out the intensive labour that was required. Thus, the Triangular Trade system was devised, carrying slaves, cash crops and manufactured goods between West Africa, the Caribbean or American colonies and the colonial powers of Europe. The African slaves were essential for producing the crops grown in the colonies that were exported to Europe. European goods were in turn used to purchase African slaves who were brought on the dreadful so-called Middle Passage to the Americas.

As everywhere, the conditions in which slaves lived and worked were appalling. By 1788, Hispaniola was supplying half of the world's coffee needs but slaves lived in windowless huts, were malnourished, brutalised and grossly overworked. As one late eighteenth century French traveller noted:

> I do not know if coffee and sugar are essential to the happiness of Europe, but I know well that these two products have accounted for the unhappiness of two great regions of the world: America [the Caribbean] has been depopulated so as to have land on which to plant them; Africa has been depopulated so as to have the people to cultivate them.

This description by the former slave, Pompée Valentin Vastey, secretary to King Henry I of Haiti, of slaves' treatment at the hands of their French masters demonstrates the true horror:

> Have they not hung men with heads downward, drowned them in sacks, crucified them on planks, buried them alive, crushed them in mortars? Have they not forced them to eat shit? And, after having flayed them with the lash, have they not cast them alive to be devoured by worms, or onto anthills, or lashed them to stakes in the swamp to be devoured by mosquitoes? Have they not thrown them into boiling cauldrons of cane syrup?

Eventually, the anger of the slaves boiled over and, in 1791, they revolted in Haiti (Hispaniola) and then, over the following few years, across the Caribbean. The Haitian revolt was the only successful slave rebellion in history, lasting for 12 years, and witnessing the emergence of the charismatic ex-slave and revolutionary leader, Toussaint Louverture (1743-1803). Of course, as the revolution in Haiti progressed, coffee harvests suffered, declining by 45 per cent from what they had been in 1789. In 1801, in order to breathe new life into coffee exports, Louverture introduced a system known as *fermage* which was no less than state slavery. Workers were forced to work in state-owned plantations for long hours and minimal wages. On the plus side, they were no longer subject to torture and physical violence and they enjoyed a degree of medical care. That year, however, Napoleon Bonaparte sent troops to Haiti in an ultimately unsuccessful attempt to regain power. The coffee plantations were once again abandoned and the harvests were a disaster. It is said that, on learning of the defeat of his forces, Napoleon shouted, 'Damn coffee! Damn colonies!' The rebellion was eventually successful but coffee never regained its former position in Haiti.

The gap in the market left by the island was filled by the Dutch East India Company who brought their beans from Java to the world market. But the labour for the production of the coffee crop was that of slaves, more than a million of them, brought in from Ambon, Ternate, Bali, Borneo, Bengal, Madagascar and a number of other places, and sold and resold on a daily basis. Not until the 1860 publication of *Max Havelaar: Or the Coffee Auctions of the Dutch Trading Company* by Multatuli (pen name of Eduard

Douwes Dekker, (1820-87)) did Dutch people realise the truth about their country's colonialism and the dreadful price many people paid so that Dutch people could relax with a cup of coffee. Multatuli wrote:

> Strangers came from the West who made themselves lords of his [the indigenous person's] land, forcing him to grow coffee for pathetic wages. *Famine?* In rich, fertile, blessed Java – *famine?* Yes, reader. Only a few years ago, whole districts died of starvation. Mothers offered their children for sale to obtain food. Mothers ate their children.

As Dekker also points out, labourers were forced to work for Dutch landowners at the expense of their own crops and wages were often withheld. However, slavery in the growth of coffee is not an evil that can be simply consigned to the past. A recent investigation by the Thomson Reuters Foundation has revealed that an increasing percentage of coffee exports from Brazil is produced using forced labour. According to this investigation, this includes coffee that is certified as slavery-free and that is sold by some of the world's largest coffee shop businesses. The majority of this modern-day slavery is concentrated in the Minas Gerais region, the southeastern state from which more than half of Brazil's entire coffee crop comes.

It is said that Brazilian coffee labourers are often trafficked, work for little or no pay, live in appalling conditions and are involved in debt-bondage. They have no contracts, are exposed to dangerous pesticides and lack protective equipment. Child slave labour is prevalent, children as young as six years old often having to work. This extends beyond Brazil, of course. In Honduras, up to 40 per cent of the workers are children and they and the women also employed are paid even less than adult male workers.

'The poor worker of the East End never knows what it is to eat good, wholesome meat or fruit – in fact, he rarely eats meat or fruit at all; while the skilled workman has nothing to boast of in the way of what he eats. Judging from the coffee-houses, which is a fair criterion, they never know in all their lives what tea, coffee, or cocoa tastes like. The slops and water-witcheries of the coffee-houses, varying only in sloppiness and witchery, never even approximate or suggest what you and I are accustomed to drink as tea and coffee.'

Jack London, *The People of the Abyss*

6

Coffee in the Nineteenth Century

War and Coffee

The inexorable growth of coffee consumption in the nineteenth century was the result of several factors. Firstly, there was the emergence of Brazil as the leading grower and exporter of coffee, making it accessible and affordable for all. Secondly, the explosion in consumption in the United States and northern Europe created a huge demand. The revolution in transport, with the growth of railways, the growth of ports and the replacement of sail by steam made possible transport of the product from the plantations to the ports and then onwards by sea, ensuring that costs remained stable while output increased. American consumption skyrocketed in the nineteenth century by virtue of reduced shipping costs, an efficient transportation system and a sophisticated marketing network that made coffee, for the first time in the United States, a mass-produced and mass-consumed product.

In 1806, three years into the Napoleonic Wars when

the French Empire and its allies fought against a coalition of various European powers, led and financed by Great Britain, the French emperor, Napoleon I, instituted the Continental System, effectively a large-scale embargo of British trade. He also declared that the days when a nation needed colonial possessions were over. 'Today we must become manufacturers,' he announced. 'We shall make everything ourselves!' It was an initiative that did not do a great deal of economic harm to Britain, but it spawned many agricultural and industrial innovations, one of which was the discovery that sweetener could be extracted from sugar beet grown in Europe, thus putting paid to a reliance on cane sugar from the Caribbean.

Coffee was, of course, a problem and, as has happened many times since, especially during times of war, chicory was used as a substitute. Chicory is a European herb, a type of endive, grown mainly as a forage crop for livestock. When it is roasted and ground, it produces a substance that has the appearance of coffee and, brewed in hot water, it can produce a dark, bitter liquid that is a bit like the beverage but delivers none of the aroma, flavour or invigorating properties that the caffeine in real coffee does. In the Napoleonic era, the French had no choice but to develop a liking for chicory 'coffee'. In fact, even after the demise of the Continental System, in 1814, many carried on adulterating their coffee with chicory and today there are a number of brands that sell it as a healthy alternative to the real thing. After the conflicts of the first 15 years of the nineteenth century, Amsterdam once again took its position as the hub for the trading of coffee. The price was initially quite low, but increased demand for the drink across Europe brought about sharp price increases. This led to coffee farmers planting new trees, and large tracts of the Amazon rain forest, for instance, were replaced with coffee bushes.

In 1823, it looked as if France and Spain might go to war over France's efforts to restore the absolutist King Ferdinand VII to the Spanish throne. This was when the new plantations were maturing and being harvested for the first time. Presuming that the sea routes to the coffee-producing nations would be closed, thus affecting supplies, European importers panic-bought coffee beans, causing the price to rise sharply. However, there was no war and the first major Brazilian crop of coffee beans was harvested. With such a huge amount of coffee beans on the market, prices plummeted and coffee businesses failed across Europe. Wealthy importers lost everything and hundreds committed suicide.

Coffee was now an international commodity, the value of which could be affected by politics, the weather, warring nations and pure speculation. For Latin America, it would change everything towards the end of the nineteenth century – its politics, its economy and its ecology.

Coffee and Slavery in Brazil

By the start of the nineteenth century, coffee was being consumed across Europe, but there were concerns that there would be insufficient to provide for the European's coffee fix. The loss of Haiti's coffee production was a major blow to the industry and it was evident that another source for the coffee bean had to be found. It turned out to be a huge country in South America.

In the second half of the nineteenth century, Brazil would become dominant in the world of coffee production. The influence of this period on the consumption of coffee was extraordinary because not only did Brazil produce a huge amount but the coffee it produced was cheap, making it affordable to the working class of the United States and Europe.

It was only in 1821 and 1822, when the Spanish and Portuguese colonies of Brazil and Latin America freed themselves from colonial hegemony that coffee became important to them. In November 1807, Napoleon's troops had taken Lisbon, the Portuguese capital, forcing the Portuguese royal family to flee the country on ships provided by the Royal Navy. They sailed to Brazil, disembarking at Rio de Janeiro where King John VI (Portugal, r. 1816-26: Brazil (king) r. 1816-22; (titular emperor) r. 1825-26) proclaimed that Brazil was a kingdom and that he was its king. He championed agriculture in his new kingdom, growing new varieties of coffee in his Royal Botanical Gardens in Rio and sending seedlings out to Brazilian coffee planters.

Coffee was not native to the Americas and the first coffee bush in Brazil had been planted by Francisco de Melo Palheta in the state of Pará in 1727. The Portuguese had been trying to obtain coffee seeds from French Guyana, but the governor of the colony was reluctant to let them have the seeds. Palheta, who had been dispatched to French Guyana to help resolve a border dispute, seduced the wife of the governor and persuaded her to give him some seeds.

Decades later, countries across Latin America broke free from their colonial rulers, firstly Venezuela, Mexico and Colombia, followed by other South and Central American countries. In 1822, Brazil freed itself from Portugal when John VI's son, Pedro I (Emperor of Brazil, r. 1822-31; King of Portugal, r. 1826), whom John had left behind as regent when he returned to Portugal in 1820, declared himself Emperor. He ruled until abdicating in favour of his 5-year-old son, Pedro II (r. 1831-89) and it was during this Pedro's 58-year-long rule that Brazil became synonymous with coffee. Along the way, however, the country paid a huge human and ecological cost.

Brazil is enormous, the world's fifth biggest country, and takes up almost half of South America. Settled by the Portuguese in 1500, its beauties were extolled 60 years later by a Jesuit priest who wrote: 'If there is a paradise here on earth, I would say it is Brazil'.

Sadly, the sugar plantations that were established in the seventeenth and eighteenth centuries were created on the principle of the large *fazenda* (plantation), owned and run by members of the wealthy elite. As elsewhere, the labour force was made up of slaves brought in from Africa who endured intolerable living and working conditions. Once transported to these plantations, slaves generally lived for only seven years and, chillingly, it was cheaper to bring in new slaves than it was to look after the health of existing ones. Added to this was the fact that the cultivation of sugarcane turned much of the lush northeast of the country into dried-up savannah.

Meanwhile, the cultivation of coffee was growing in the southeast of the country, since it was better suited to the more temperate climate of the mountainous region near Rio de Janeiro. Once this region had been mined for gold and diamonds, and with those minerals exhausted, people turned to farming coffee. Slaves who had previously looked for precious minerals were taught how to harvest coffee beans and the success of the coffee bush in the region led to an increase in the number of slaves being brought in. By 1819, the population of Brazil was 3.6 million and at least a third were enslaved Africans. Six years later, the proportion of slaves in Brazil had risen to a staggering 56 per cent of the population.

Britain outlawed slavery in 1807 and, after that date, Royal Navy ships tried to intercept the slave ships that continued to sail the Middle Passage. It was a difficult task, though. Brazil tried to placate Britain by making slavery illegal in 1831, but it was no more than a gesture and the evil trade carried on. Finally, as British warships began to enjoy success against slave ships, the Brazilian government banned the importation of slaves. This was little comfort, however, to the two million who were already in bondage in the country. On the back of their labour, coffee growers became the wealthiest people in Brazil, creating huge estates known as *latifundia*, worked by hundreds of slaves. Work began with prayers at four in the morning and continued until seven in the evening. Even then their labour was not finished – until nine they worked in the household or toiled at the mill or elsewhere on the estate. Men and women were then locked up in separate quarters. It was seventeen hours of back-breaking labour and it was little wonder that not many slaves survived more than seven years of it.

Of course, there were benign plantation-owners who treated their slaves with some compassion, but many indulged in beatings and murders, none of which interested the authorities. The children of slaves were sold to other plantations and never saw their parents again. They were basically treated like animals and were considered less than human. But, of course, there was always the fear of reprisals, and owners and white managers rarely went unarmed.

Slavery was practised in Brazil for longer than any other Western Hemisphere nation but the government finally passed the Law of Free Birth in 1871. Slavery had been causing social tensions between the country's conservatives and liberals and this law provided freedom to all new-born children of slaves. It marked the start of an abolition movement in Brazil but not many were freed and there were still more than a million slaves. Slavery was finally abolished in 1888 with the Lei Áurea – the Golden Law, signed into law by Isabel, Princess Imperial of Brazil (1846-1921) who was acting as regent while Pedro II was in Europe.

The aggressive cultivation of coffee in the Rio area throughout the nineteenth century brought forest decimation and natural resources were exhausted. This led to a move to the south and west, to the plateaus of São Paolo which became the hub of the burgeoning Brazilian coffee industry. And coffee was making people very rich, as prices rose in the 1860s and 1870s. A railway was built from Santos on the coast to the coffee-growing region and, by 1889, there were 6,000 miles of track servicing the coffee regions and connecting with Santos or Rio. In 1874, communications with Europe were opened up with the laying of a cable across the Atlantic, making it easier to do business. The arrival of ships powered by steam also contributed to the coffee trade's advancement.

After 1850, planters encouraged European immigrants to come to work on their plantations, replacing the slaves. They were typically given a house, some land on which to grow food for themselves and a set number of coffee trees to cultivate and harvest. The debt these *colonos* – settlers – had incurred for travelling to Brazil was to be paid off, as well as other advance payments they would inevitably have had to request. It was simply debt bondage, especially as the immigrants were forbidden from leaving the plantation while the debt remained unpaid. As this could take many years, it was a terrible imposition.

This new form of slavery eased somewhat in 1884 when plantation owners persuaded the government to pay the transportation costs. This encouraged more immigrants, mostly poor Italians, more than a million of whom arrived between 1884 and 1914 to sweat on the coffee plantations. The conditions were still pretty bad and armed guards were often used to protect plantation owners.

At the end of the nineteenth century, coffee production soared in Brazil. From 5.5 million bags in 1890, it rose to more than 16 million in 1901. By that time, more than 500 million coffee bushes had been planted in the state of São Paolo and the world was inundated with Brazilian coffee. Of course, the reliance on one crop did a great deal of damage to the country, and valuable reserves had to be spent on importing ordinary foodstuffs, such as flour.

Coffee in Victorian Britain

Coffee was extremely popular in nineteenth century Britain, especially amongst working-class labourers. Testimony to this can be found in *London Labour and the London Poor* by the social reformer, Henry Mayhew (1812-87):

> It is less easy to describe the diet of costermongers [street vendors of fruit and vegetables] than it is to describe that of many of the labouring classes, for their diet, so to speak, is an 'out-of-door' diet. They breakfast at a 'coffee-stall', and (if all their means have been expended in purchasing their stock, and none of it yet to be sold) they expend on the meal only one penny, reserved for the purchase. For this sum they can procure a small cup of coffee, and two 'thin' (that is to say two thin slices of bread and butter).

Mayhew claims that street vendors of tea and coffee were rare on the streets of Britain before 1840 – 'coffee was in little demand, even amongst smaller tradesmen and farmers' – but 20 years later they seem to have been everywhere and he records more than 300 coffee stalls in the streets of the capital, mostly owned and run by women. He complains that the coffee was usually adulterated with chicory or by what he called baked and ground 'saccharine roots' such as carrots. These stalls, providing the working classes with takeaway breakfasts, were generally located in the poorer districts, places such as Covent Garden in London, at the time home to a busy market but also to prostitution.

The coffee stall would offer coffee, and, ostensibly, tea and cocoa, for sale from cans. Also on sale were bread and butter, currant cake, sandwiches and boiled eggs. Being England, one would imagine that tea was what was principally sold. Mayhew contradicts this: 'Coffee is the article mostly sold at the stalls; indeed, there is scarcely one stall in a hundred that is supplied with tea, and not more than a dozen in all London that furnish cocoa'. The beans for the coffee were purchased from a grocery store and the women who owned the stalls would roast and grind them themselves, adding whatever they needed to bulk it out with possibly a little burnt sugar to ensure the correct dark brown colour.

In the middle of the nineteenth century, Europeans and North Americans still purchased their coffee unroasted. The beans were sold, more often than not, from the bags in which they had been shipped from their source and were ground by mortar and pestle and roasted at home. Initially, they were sold by coffee houses, but as time went on, they began to appear on market stalls and were sold by street peddlers. Pre-ground coffee was also available at the time. At home, coffee was roasted over fires in long-handled pans and when the quality of the original beans was good, the coffee was worth the trouble. The problem was, though, that the coffee beans available for purchase were often not of a very high standard. Conditions on board the ships on which they were transported were paramount in the standard of the product that was eventually offloaded in Europe or America. Also critical was whatever commodity the coffee beans were stored next to in the ship's hold. If it was pepper, for instance, the coffee beans would be greatly affected by that. In the damp conditions on board, mildew could also be a problem, but through time lessons were learned and precautions were taken to ensure that it was stored securely.

By mid-century, wages were increasing, meaning that families had greater disposable income to lavish on luxuries. Packaged goods were also becoming increasingly common, mass production replacing domestic production of everyday items. And mass production meant mass consumption. Speciality shops began to replace stalls and peddlers and these served everyone, not just the middle and upper classes. Bulk goods were packaged in the shop and were sold for a fixed price. So, coffee, with more countries growing and exporting, began to grow in popularity and was affordable for a larger percentage of the population. In grocery shops, which were often filled with the enticing aroma of coffee, it was now routinely offered for sale pre-roasted and already ground. This took away all the drudgery of preparing an enlivening cup. As a consequence, sales soared.

Added to the convenience factor was the greater ease of distribution up and down the country, made possible by the inexorable expansion of the railways and the change from sail to steam on the world's oceans. Industrial roasters were processing huge quantities of beans that, by the start of the twentieth century, were ready for distribution to shops throughout Britain.

Coffee in the USA in the Nineteenth Century

Coffee had once been prohibitively expensive for Americans, as it had to be transported such long distances – from Turkey or Indonesia, for example. But, with islands such as Haiti, Cuba and Puerto Rico, located close to the American coastline, producing coffee, the beverage became significantly more affordable and available. Certainly, the Boston Tea Party and the colonists' antipathy towards the English contributed greatly to the drinking of coffee rather than tea, but geography might also have played a large part in it. Coffee-producing regions were much closer to the United States than tea-growing ones. The hugely diverse population of the young country might also have contributed to coffee becoming its favourite beverage in preference to tea.

Coffee came into the USA by a variety of routes. The parts of America that France controlled until the early nineteenth century – Louisiana and up the Mississippi to

Canada – would have secured their coffee from the French possession, Haiti. Florida, a Spanish possession until 1822, was a short sail from the coffee plantations of Cuba, and the territories to the west would have received their coffee through Mexico which, until it started growing its own, obtained its coffee from the Antilles.

A decisive factor in establishing coffee culture in the United States was the arrival of refugees from Europe after the various revolutions across the continent in 1848. Often middle-class intellectuals from cities such as Berlin, Budapest, Prague and Vienna, they would have honed their debating skills in the vibrant and long-established coffee houses of those cities and were happy to establish similar settings in the land they now called home. Indeed, by the late nineteenth century, a staggering amount of coffee was being consumed in the United States. According to *The American Grocer*, a trade magazine of the time, in the two years from 1878 to 1880, the port of New York was the conduit for around 264 million pounds of coffee beans a year from Brazil, while San Francisco handled almost 17 million pounds of Costa Rican, Guatemalan, El Salvadorian and Nicaraguan beans. Annually, the United States was consuming 345 million pounds of coffee. In Europe, consumption could not match this – Germany drank 224 million; France, 119 million; Austria, 81 million; Netherlands, 68 million; Italy, 28 million; the Iberian Peninsula, 7 million. These figures, of course, discount smuggling which was fairly widespread and they also ignore processing and exporting to other countries, such as was done in Hamburg and Amsterdam.

Nonetheless, the United States' important position in coffee consumption is clear.

Coffee's American miracle in the nineteenth century was also a consequence of US government policy. It was the only place in the world where, for a period, coffee was imported tax-free. In 1812, duty on coffee was set at ten cents a pound but, by 1814, it was five cents. Then for ten years from 1832, it was all but free. The growth in per capita consumption as a result was plain to see. In 1783, it was just one-eighteenth of a pound. By 1880, it had risen to nine pounds. And in that time, imports of coffee had grown 2,400 per cent. By the turn of the century, Americans were consuming 13 pounds a head annually which amounted to 40 per cent of the world's coffee. Fifty per cent of the growth in consumption of coffee in the nineteenth century was down to the United States.

Technology and Emerging Brands

Industrialisation had arrived in the United States and Europe and, like many other products and commodities, coffee benefited greatly from it. Roasting and brewing equipment were developed. France, concerned with the best means of brewing, and Germany with its growing engineering credentials, competed with the other great engineering nation, Great Britain to create the best. Countless patents were issued for new equipment guaranteed to make a better brew of coffee or to further industrialise the process of coffee production. All of these were targeted to greatly increase the market for coffee.

Progress was most noticeable in the United States. Where once coffee had been roasted in small, local roasteries that provided the raw ingredients for local coffee houses and grocery stores, there were now factories that did everything, from roasting, blending and grinding to packaging and distribution. Of course, any local quirks were ironed out and the product was now standardised, each pack tasting and looking the same. Coffee was being taken to the masses and out beyond the cities to the American hinterland. The story of Folgers Coffee – one of the great American brands and now the largest-selling ground coffee in the United States – is an exemplar of the industrialisation process and of just how popular coffee was becoming.

Folgers was founded by William H Bovee (1823-94) in San Francisco in 1850 as the Pioneer Steam Coffee and Spice Mills. He had spotted the opportunity to provide Californians with roasted, ground coffee, instead of the green coffee beans that they had to roast and grind themselves. The company did very well, selling coffee and condiments to the thousands of prospectors from all over the world who were arriving in San Francisco before heading out to the goldfields to seek their fortune. During the Gold Rush, the city grew from just a few hundred residents in 1848 to 36,000 in 1864 and the Pioneer Steam Coffee and Spice Mills had to expand rapidly to keep up with the growth. When he had founded the company, William Bovee had hired a carpenter, James A Folger (1835-89), to help in the construction of his mill. Aged just 15, Folger had journeyed from his hometown, Nantucket, to California in search of his fortune. He saved during his first year at the company and was able to invest these savings in the company before heading out to the goldfields to prospect for gold. On his trip he took samples of the coffee and spices the company sold, visiting grocery stores *en route* and soliciting orders. Returning to San Francisco in 1865, he became a full partner in the company and, six years later, he bought out the other partners, renaming the business J A Folger & Co.

When the company started, its processes were very basic. Roasting and grinding were carried out using hand-cranked machines. They started selling their ground coffee in tins that sold in quantities to the prospectors who needed it as an energy-giving stimulant and also as a means of keeping hunger at bay as they worked. It was successful and the business was soon forced to relocate to larger premises. Steam-powered machinery was introduced. By 1855, Folgers coffee was being distributed throughout California and in a few decades it had become a nationally recognised brand.

Another great coffee brand, Maxwell House, had similarly humble beginnings. In 1884, a former schoolteacher, Joel Owsley Cheek (1852-1935), moved to Nashville, Tennessee where he met a British coffee broker, Roger Nolley Smith. Smith was a coffee expert and during the next few years, the two men worked together to create the perfect blend of coffee. In 1892, Cheek persuaded the food buyer at the Maxwell House Hotel in Nashville to try 20 pounds of their blend. After a few days, supplies of Cheek's blend had been exhausted and the hotel returned to using its customary blend. But after the hotel's guests complained that they preferred the coffee they had been drinking before, the Maxwell House Hotel began buying Cheek's blend exclusively. This encouraged Cheek to leave his job as a coffee broker and set up a wholesale grocery distribution business, the Nashville Coffee and Manufacturing Company, specialising, as the company name suggests, in coffee. At the heart of the business was their coffee, now branded Maxwell House Coffee. The company name later changed to the Cheek-Neale Coffee Company and in 1928 it was sold for around $40 million.

Following the American Civil War that had devastated the country, the United States experienced a period of huge economic growth and staggering national reconstruction, including the completion in 1869 of the transcontinental railway. This meant that goods could be shipped from one side of the country to the other in just days where previously it would have taken months. This period of expansion brought further industrialisation of coffee and the emergence of visionary individuals who saw the opportunities that lay in the tens of thousands of people flooding into the western territories in search of a new future. These entrepreneurs envisaged a national network of coffee distribution for sale in grocery stores in the West.

During the nineteenth century, a number of patents were issued in Europe and the United States for commercial roasters that could roast large amounts of coffee. In the 1850s, however, roasting at home remained the most popular method. Thus, devices for roasting at home were devised and marketed, such as a spherical roaster, developed in Cincinnati in 1849, which was fitted into a burner opening on the top of a wood-fired kitchen stove. Most simply spread their beans on a metal sheet in the oven or stirred them in a pan over a fire but the American roasting industry was revolutionised by innovations patented by Jabez Burns in the 1860s.

In 1864, the Arbuckle brothers, working at their family's wholesale grocery business, made a major breakthrough, creating a one-pound paper bag of roasted coffee, hermetically sealed and labelled. The brand they created was Ariosa and, within about 20 years, it was the top-selling coffee brand in the United States. In the 1860s, John Arbuckle invented a process – using a mixture of sugar and eggs – for keeping roasted coffee beans fresh during weeks of transport and storage. As his coffee became increasingly successful, the Arbuckles required a lot of sugar and it was proving to be expensive. The solution was to open their own sugar refinery. This irritated the Havemeyer family who had immigrated to New York from Germany in the early nineteenth century, had created the American Sugar Refining Company, and had become the major player in the organisation known as the Sugar Trust which controlled the price of sugar and its distribution throughout the country. In order to cut the Arbuckles down to size for muscling in on their industry, the Havemeyers, with others in the Sugar Trust, spent two million dollars on the purchase of an Ohio coffee roastery, the Woolson Spice Company. Huge sums were lavished on marketing their Lion Coffee brand, even selling at a loss.

The outcome of this war between two coffee companies was an investigation in 1897 into Havemeyer's and, ultimately, into the American coffee trade by the New York State Legislative Committee. While Havemeyer testified before the committee that the coffee business offered good profits, Arbuckle insisted that Lion Coffee must be losing between $500 and $1,000 a day and that the coffee business was no longer, as a result, worth being in.

As ever, the customer was the loser. Packaged coffee was now available everywhere. One investigating journalist was told by a source in the industry that the practice was to sell good quality coffee in attractive packaging initially, but once the brand had been established and sales were good, the customer would find that he or she was paying for the marketing gimmicks – gifts and tokens – while the quality of the coffee went down. There was an antipathy against packaged coffee, he claimed, that led retailers to empty the coffee from the bags and blend it with better grades of coffee to provide a better and low-priced product.

Coffee in Late Nineteenth Century Europe

Café culture blossomed across Europe towards the end of the nineteenth century, particularly in Germany, France and the Austro-Hungarian Empire. Everywhere, cities were changing, modernising and getting rid of the disease-ridden slums and dank alleys of the past. Paris, Berlin, Prague, Budapest and Vienna all underwent huge renovations, their centres being rebuilt and adorned by magnificent wide boulevards. Lining these extravagant thoroughfares were numerous lavishly appointed cafés. These gentrified cafés and others, less ornate, became the meeting places for the young artists and writers who were contributing to the artistic explosion that marked the period that came to be known as the Belle Époque.

We are very aware of the famous cafés where now-celebrated artists, writers and musicians spent their downtime, but cafés were important for everyone, especially in Central Europe, in Budapest, Vienna and Prague, cities that had become home to a great, swirling, multicultural mass of peoples from the east, from Crimea, Bosnia, Ukraine and other places. Trades and professions had their own favourite spots. The Hungarian-British writer, George Mikes (1912-87) described the cafés of this period:

Every profession used to have its own coffeehouse and its *stammtisch*, the regular table of regular guests. Every shade, faction or sub-group of each profession had its own coffeehouse… In addition to the well-known tables of artists, there were coffeehouses for textile merchants, dentists, horse-dealers, politicians and pickpockets among many others. The world of criminals was as much subdivided as every other sphere. A mere pickpocket would not be accepted by the table of self-respecting safe-breakers any more than a small money-lender would be tolerated at the table of top bankers…

He enumerates 28 different types of coffee drinks in one particular coffee house in Vienna and also registers understandable surprise that Vienna became home to the coffee house rather than Budapest which, after all, had once been part of the Ottoman Empire. But the Magyars had never really taken to coffee. In fact, a saying in Hungarian speaks of how bemused they were by the Turks' love of the beverage: 'The black soup is yet to come'. Nonetheless, they grew to enjoy it and the environment it engendered in the setting of a café.

The cafés of Paris were an entirely different thing. Central European cafés were all about coffee in its multifarious forms. The Parisian bohemian and frequenter of cafés was more concerned with alcohol and coffee came as an added extra. And, of course, the alcohol was often in the form of the notorious absinthe. Brandy was another firm favourite. In the grander establishments, the well-dressed elite showed off, with snooty waiters dressed in tuxedos, sneering at all and sundry. But there were also countless small cafés where a worker might stop on the way to work for a cup of coffee and a croissant, and perhaps even a small glass of something alcoholic to kick-start the day. Perhaps later, or at the weekend, the worker might join other ordinary Parisians in reading a newspaper or discussing the events of the day with acquaintances in a friendly, convivial atmosphere. Interestingly, the Paris that existed after Baron Georges-Eugene Haussmann (1809-91) had renovated it, was a democratic city, in that the classes all lived together in a kind of vertical arrangement – the middle class occupied the ground floor and each successive floor above was home to an increasingly lower class until one reached the attic which was home to the very poorest people. Areas were, therefore, mixed in terms of class and occupation and this could be seen in the cafés that served these areas.

In these cafés, coffee was a simple drink, served either black or white, and it features, along with the equipment used to make it, in a number of Impressionist paintings. One famous artists' café was Café Guerbois on Avenue de Clichy, a meeting place for bohemians of all colours. At the time, the main personage was Édouard Manet, a pivotal figure in the transition from Realism to Impressionism. On Sundays and Thursdays, he might be joined by the writer Émile Zola, and the artists Frédéric Bazille, Henri Fantin-Latour, Edgar Degas, Claude Monet, Pierre-Auguste Renoir, Paul Cézanne, Camille Pissarro and Alfred Sisley. In some cafés, the mythology goes, bills were paid with canvasses that one day might be worth fortunes.

The Temperance Movement

In 1838, there were still 3,000 coffee houses plying their trade in London. Robert Montgomery Martin, in his book of that year, *The Past and Present State of the Tea Trade of England*, estimated that in these establishments 2,000 pounds of tea and 15,000 pounds of coffee were drunk on a daily basis. This, he notes, was an increase from a few years previously, and he suggests that this increase can be laid fairly at the door of the rapidly growing temperance movement.

This movement had sprung up in the eighteenth century when Great Britain was beset by a craze for drinking gin. The bourgeoisie, anxious for order in their rapidly growing cities, were horrified and the consumption of alcohol became a major issue. Meanwhile, in the United States, alcohol had become an essential, as water supplies were not always reliable and milk was often not available. Although initially not a great issue, by the nineteenth century, it was becoming a problem. Temperance societies began to appear, often run by churches. The movement began to be organised on a national level in the 1820s, and the emphasis was on avoiding hard spirits, rather than all alcohol. The Evangelical Protestant religious revival in America of the 1820s and 1830s, known as the Second Great Awakening, also promoted temperance. However, the movement still consisted mainly of people who attended church. In England, about the same time, temperance societies were being formed and the movement began to spread around the world.

As towns and cities became more urbanised and social problems increased, the more formal and certainly stricter form of temperance known as teetotalism began to be espoused. This was total abstinence from all alcoholic beverages. In Britain, teetotalism began in Preston in 1833. The Catholic temperance movement was launched in 1838 and the British electoral reform movement, Chartism, even had a branch that advocated temperance. The Chartists believed that, if working men abstained from alcohol, it would oblige the elite to acknowledge that they were responsible enough to be given the vote.

Many municipalities began to prohibit the sale of alcohol and alcohol consumption in the United States decreased by half between 1830 and 1840. In both Britain and America this could only be of benefit to purveyors of other drinks, including, of course, coffee. In Britain, 'coffee taverns' were promoted by temperance advocates, associating them in the minds of the working class with pubs. They did not last long but brought coffee to many who had never drunk it before. A pamphlet of the time – *Practical Hints on Management of Coffee Houses* – gave advice on how to establish one of these establishments. At the time, British industry was making strenuous efforts to ensure that its workforce was sober and arrived at work punctually. Old habits had to be broken, especially the practice of workers drinking to excess on a Sunday and taking Monday off to recover. Coffee taverns were, therefore, the answer, providing a meeting place for the workers where they could not access alcohol. There was little doubt that the promoters of such places saw them as morally uplifting and improving. The leaflet suggested space being set aside for meetings and for music to be performed. Newspapers were to be provided.

But the reforming nature of the coffee tavern and the temperance movement in general often aroused suspicion in working men. As many recognised, drinking to excess was merely a symptom of the greater problems of Victorian times – poor sanitation, harsh working conditions, overcrowding and poor living conditions. They resented being pontificated to by the middle and upper classes and they were antagonised by the patronising attitude shown to them. Coffee taverns faded away but coffee was now a part of working-class life.

Coffee from Africa

Coffee is best suited to the Earth's tropical zone which is delimited by the Tropic of Cancer in the Northern Hemisphere and the Tropic of Capricorn in the Southern Hemisphere. The weather is hot there, but it is not the heat that makes it suitable for growing the coffee plant. After all, coffee thrives in mountainous country or in areas that do not suffer the extremes of sunshine. Rather, it is the light of this region that has allowed it to come to be known as the Coffee Belt or the Coffee Zone. Inside that area, all coffee grown for commercial purposes can be found. The Coffee Belt incorporates the Americas – from Mexico through Central America to Brazil, the Caribbean and Hawaii; Africa – the Ivory Coast, Tanzania, Uganda, Kenya, Burundi, Cameroon, Congo, Rwanda, Guinea, Ethiopia, Togo, Zimbabwe, Nigeria, Ghana, Zambia, Malawi, Benin and Gabon; and Asia – India, Indonesia, the Philippines, Vietnam and southern China.

Towards the end of the nineteenth century, the places where coffee was being cultivated for export principally to North America and Europe greatly increased in number. There were a couple of factors that contributed to this increase in producer nations. Firstly, in the last few decades of the century, the coffee producers of the East began to be badly affected by the voracious parasite *Hemileia vastatrix*, creating a fungus known as rust. Rust is of East African origin and was first reported in Sri Lanka (formerly Ceylon) in 1867. It struck India in 1870, Sumatra in 1876, Java in 1878 and the Philippines in 1889. It would strike Africa in the twentieth century. This, obviously, reduced supplies of coffee beans, but the second factor made it a real problem – or, for new producers, an opportunity. Technological advances had vastly expanded the market for coffee and this provided ample encouragement for new areas of the Tropical Zone to be opened up for the cultivation of the coffee bean. It was also a spur to the older producing countries to modernise their production processes.

The so-called 'Scramble for Africa', when European powers – Belgium, France, Britain, Germany, Portugal and France – carved out large chunks of Africa for themselves, also had a bearing on the history of coffee cultivation. This plundering of an entire continent was dressed up by European politicians as a way of 'civilising' the indigenous peoples. This was to be done with the Bible, education and, if those failed, the Gatling gun. Whole swathes of land were laid waste and millennia-old cultures disappeared. But African colonialism was beneficial for coffee as new varieties of the coffee plant were discovered. The plantations that were created in Africa at that time benefited hugely from the technological know-how and technical skills that had recently been developed. Much could be learned from growing coffee in Africa.

There was also development in Central America and a number of countries of that region even offered incentives to people to emigrate and work in the coffee trade there. Passage was paid, grants were given and financial help was provided for the first weeks in the country. There were also inducements for individuals as well as companies who wanted to organise settlements that would produce coffee. Several persecuted religious groups from Europe availed themselves of this opportunity. Germans, especially, took advantage of these inducements and they settled in large numbers, eventually becoming an important part of the burgeoning Central American coffee industry.

'Starbucks represents something beyond a cup of coffee.'

Howard Schultz, former CEO of Starbucks

Coffee in the Twentieth and Twenty-First Centuries

Instant Coffee

The idea of an instant form of coffee goes back a long way. Convenience was one good reason, especially back in the days when making a cup of coffee – roasting and grinding the beans – was a time-consuming process. Occasionally, the requisite implements were not to hand – a fire had to be lit and the roasting pan and grinder had to be within reach. Coffee ceased to be an infrequent luxury and turned into a daily necessity but making it on a daily basis was a grind, on every level. For traders, if the bean was removed from the process, then its provenance ceased to be much of an issue. This had become a problem as people's tastes, regarding coffee, became more sophisticated. They understood the difference between a smooth Mocha and a harsh Brazil. Not that the labels always meant much, anyway; mislabelling was endemic in the coffee trade. If the essence of coffee could be sold, there would no longer be the problem of storage. It could be stored for as long as necessary without a consequent deterioration in quality. Above all, it could be drunk anywhere, at any time, without the need for special equipment or, indeed, much effort.

There was a lot to be said for an instant form of coffee, therefore, and those in the industry recognised the potential it would give to reach new, untapped markets, to make their beverage available to all. After all, it would not be aficionados who would be interested. They would still want to indulge in their coffee ritual and would not be prepared to sacrifice quality in the name of convenience. Instant coffee would, instead, be the beverage for the masses who had no interest in the origins of the bean that was flavouring their drink. They had never encountered a really good cup of coffee. All they wanted was the warm buzz of caffeine that coffee delivered.

Instant coffee's popularity is quite incredible. There are few – if any – other examples of a pseudo-product becoming pre-eminent in its market. There had been previous efforts. In 1771, the first patent for a coffee compound was filed in England and, during the American Civil War, the Union army produced a concentrated coffee, condensed milk and sugar mixture called Essence of Coffee. A spoonful was added to a cup of hot water. Unfortunately, instead of, as the label claimed, being 'more wholesome than pure coffee', the result was a thick, brown sludge often compared to axle grease. It was soon discontinued.

A Scottish drink, Camp Coffee, a coffee and chicory syrup or essence, appeared in the 1880s, created in Glasgow in 1885 by Campbell Paterson (1851-1927) for his company, R Paterson & Son. The company primarily made fruit cordials, but Paterson developed his coffee syrup to help people who could not afford the expensive equipment for making coffee. Legend suggests that it was created as an instant coffee to give soldiers the opportunity to quickly brew a cup of the beverage while on military duties. This was demonstrated on the label which depicted a Gordon Highlander at the time of the British Raj in India. He is seated in front of a bell tent and is being served by a Sikh soldier who is holding a tray with a bottle of Camp essence and a jug of hot water. At the top of the tent flies a flag on which is the legend, 'Ready Aye Ready', the slogan for the drink but also the motto of the 59th Scinde Rifles (Frontier Force) of the British Indian Army.

Instant, or soluble coffee is said to have been patented in France in 1881 by Alphonse Allais (1854-1905), but Allais was a humourist and was the creator of many ridiculous inventions, including a fish tank made of frosted glass for shy fish. His creation of instant coffee, therefore, may have been a hoax on his part. More seriously, however, in 1890, a New Zealander, David Strang used his patented 'Dry-Hot-Air' process to make Strang's Coffee. A Japanese-American scientist named Satori Kato, who was working in Chicago, had already devised a soluble tea. His instant coffee was exhibited at the 1901 Pan-American Exposition in Buffalo, New York, the event at which US President William McKinley was assassinated. Kato's coffee was used on the 1901 Arctic Expedition funded by American industrialist,

William Ziegler (1843-1905). Faust Instant Coffee, made by the entrepreneur and inventor, Cyrus F Blanke's CF Blanke Coffee and Tea Co, followed a few years later, winning the Grand Prize and gold medal at the St Louis World's Fair in 1904. Its advertising slogan was ambitious, to say the least: 'The best on earth or anywhere else'.

A Belgian immigrant, George Washington (1871-1946), an inventor and businessman, arrived in New York in 1897 and worked in several different fields before inventing a process for making instant coffee. Legend has it that he came up with the idea while he was living in Guatemala, after noticing some dried powder on the edge of a silver coffee pot. He founded the G Washington Coffee Refining Company to mass-produce it in 1910, marketing it as Red E Coffee. Advertising focused on the convenience of the product, also claiming that it was better for the digestion than normal coffee. However, it was reported that his coffee had an unpleasant taste. Sold to American Home Products in 1943, three years before Washington's death, Washington's instant coffee was produced until 1961.

The popularity of instant coffee arose from two different factors – an economic crisis in Brazil and war. In 1929, Brazil had huge stocks of coffee languishing unsold in its warehouses. In order to try to restore stability by safeguarding the falling prices of the forthcoming harvest, the government had little option but to order that the excess beans be disposed of. They were burned or tossed into the ocean. Inevitably, many fortunes were lost as a result. This particular cloud had a silver lining for the Swiss condensed milk and chocolate manufacturer, Nestlé. In 1866, the Anglo-Swiss Condensed Milk Company was founded. A year later, Henri Nestlé developed a breakthrough baby food, *farine lactée*, which combined cow's milk, wheat flour and sugar. The Nestlé Group was established by a merger of these two businesses in 1905. Nestlé carefully analysed the global coffee market and came to the conclusion that it would be wise to invest in the cheap coffee that was available from Brazil if they could succeed in doing what no one had yet done – create coffee in a soluble form that tasted good. They certainly had the technology, as they had already devised a technique for dehydrating milk for use in making milk chocolate and other powdered dairy products. Max Morgenthaler (1901-80) was appointed to head the development project with the objective of making a coffee extract powder that would be better by far than any instant coffee yet produced. It took the young chemist seven years to perfect his process which involved spray-drying liquid coffee under high pressure to create a rich, soluble powder that was the first really enjoyable instant coffee. They called it Nescafé and launched it on 1 April 1938.

The timing was important, in that it was launched just before the start of the Second World War. Wars were important to the development of coffee. G Washington's Red E Coffee was drunk by the US Army during both World Wars and, indeed, the First World War was the first conflict during which coffee became an essential part of a soldier's rations. Naturally, conditions in the trenches made instant coffee the ideal solution. The US Army, therefore, began to place large orders for instant coffee, purchasing 37,000 pounds a day by the war's end. Unfortunately, the desire for coffee made in an instant died with the end of the war and the instant coffee industry entered a decline after 1918. It would take another conflict, the Second World War, to create the need for it once more and Nescafé would become a staple item for Americans during the conflict. In fact, by 1941, Americans were drinking more coffee than ever and the ordinary GI maintained, and indeed increased his coffee intake, consuming some 31 pounds of coffee every year of the war. The bean became a vital part of the war effort, whether on the battlefield or in the armaments factory, providing that essential and invigorating kick of caffeine that allowed people to stave off exhaustion and lack of focus. At home, it was still the traditional roasted and ground bean that was drunk, but in its instant variety it was hoovered up by the military which requisitioned almost all of its production.

So, a taste for instant developed in the war and, after 1946, its popularity increased even in countries that had never previously known it. In the United States, it began to steal market share from the traditional variety, seizing a third of the market by the late 1950s. This was partly a result of the decline in the quality of the roasted and ground variety. Soon there was, frankly, little difference between the traditional roasted and ground coffee and its instant brother. Other contributory factors were the presence of American troops, and therefore instant coffee, around the world after the war and the use of the cheaper Robusta coffee bean, providing a cheap beverage at a time when money was not in plentiful supply for most people.

Nescafé would become, effectively, the world's first truly successful global instant coffee brand. Its Swiss origins paid dividends as Switzerland was a neutral country and the company managed to avoid the political problems of distributing to Axis countries and the nations they had conquered. More importantly, however, was the supply chain that was established with Brazil. Cheap Brazilian coffee could now be processed so that it could be stored indefinitely before being sold. Thus coffee became a product for the giant corporations of the processed food industry. With their peerless organisation in handling foodstuffs and their efficiencies of cost, they were in a position to produce instant coffee on a massive scale.

Instant coffee is made by brewing a large amount of coffee and then concentrating it, using one of a variety of means – such as evaporation or low-pressure extraction. It can be spray-dried or freeze-dried. It has also been sold in a concentrated liquid form. As a result of instant's growing popularity, there has been huge investment in research into its production, as well as in advertising and marketing it, especially in Germany and Great Britain. In the United Kingdom, the big player is Nestlé which has achieved almost a monopoly through the quality of its product and extremely effective advertising. Its profit margins are also very high.

But, instant coffee is not, to the coffee lover, the real thing. Instant manufacturers are accused of trickery, such as the technique known as 'plating on'. This involves injecting the top of a jar with a simulated coffee aroma that, for the drinker, approximates the smell of fresh coffee when the lid is unscrewed and the seal broken. The instant variety contains more caffeine than roasted ground coffee. However, it provides redemption for the Robusta bean, reducing its least desirable elements.

In Great Britain, the coffee market has been dominated by instant coffee. This has been ascribed to the nation's predilection for tea and to its historic disdain for food culture of the sort that can be found in Italy and France, for example. Perhaps, though, this liking for instant coffee derives from the 1950s when Nestlé, with its brand Nescafé, and Maxwell House became fixed in the public consciousness as the only coffee British people knew and would drink. In fact, instant coffee became an aspirational drink for the nation's emerging middle classes and there was some cachet in its labour-saving quality. Advertising played a large part in this and coffee ads, especially ones for Nescafé, are held in high regard. The commercials for Nescafé Gold Blend featuring the Gold Blend couple, playing out a romance in a series of twelve 45-second spots between 1987 and 1993, were followed avidly by the British public.

Decaf

The consumption of caffeine has, down the years, been frowned upon by all sorts of well-meaning people.

Eventually, efforts were made to sell coffee from which this element had been removed. In 1895, the Post Cereal Company founder, CW Post (1854-1914) created and marketed a coffee substitute, a roasted-grain beverage that was entirely free of caffeine. Post was a student of John Harvey Kellogg (1852-1943), a nutritionist, inventor of the breakfast cereal Corn Flakes and a vehement opponent of the consumption of tea and coffee. Postum cereal beverage was made from wheat and molasses and was astutely promoted by Post, playing on consumers' concerns about caffeine with fearmongering advertising messages such as: 'It is safe to say that one person in three among coffee users has some incipient or advanced form of disease'. His product was called Postum Food Coffee, but he was eventually forced to remove the word 'Coffee' from his product packaging, because the coffee bean played no part whatsoever in its manufacture. Post's business acquired other companies, including Maxwell House in 1928, and changed its name to General Foods in 1929. Post Consumer Brands is now the third-largest breakfast cereal brand in the United States. Postum Roasted Wheat-Bran & Molasses Instant Warm Beverage is today sold by Eliza's Quest Foods.

In 1906, the Hamburg coffee merchant, Ludwig Roselius (1874-1943), founded Kaffee HAG (Handels-Aktiengesellschaft), after filing a patent three years earlier for a decaffeination process of the same name as his company. His process involved steaming coffee beans in salt water in order to open their pores before rinsing them repeatedly with the chemical compound benzene which extracted all the caffeine from the beans. Benzene has since been found to be a carcinogen, and safer solvents have replaced it. It is said that Roselius was keen to create a decaffeinated coffee because his father's death at an early age was attributed by his doctor to his addiction to caffeine. He marketed his product with the slogan, 'Always harmless, always digestible', and it was the first coffee to use the medium of the silent film for advertising. Kaffee HAG became a global brand, was purchased by General Foods in 1979 and has been owned by the Dutch company, Jacobs Douwe Egberts, since 2015.

Many others launched decaffeinated coffee brands, in both Europe and the United States, and research into the best methods continued. Caffeine makes up around 1 to 2.5 per cent of the dry weight of a coffee bean. Good quality Arabica beans contain about half the amount of caffeine found in lower quality Robusta beans. There is double the quantity per cup of instant coffee than ground and espresso surprisingly contains less because of the rapid extraction and lower weight of coffee used in making it. To decaffeinate coffee, the green beans require soaking in a solvent. As we have seen, benzene was discarded for health reasons, as was methyl chloride. Ethyl acetate was next, but in 1933, a Swiss company pioneered a method that used water as the solvent. This was developed commercially by a company named Coffex in 1980. In recent times, Kurt Zosel (1913-89) of the Max Planck Institute, introduced supercritical carbon dioxide (a fluid state of the gas where it is held at or above its critical temperature and critical pressure) as a means of safe decaffeination.

The Business of Coffee

Coffee is unlike most other crops in that it is predictable. One huge harvest is more often than not followed by a poor one. Given that it is a crop that is harvested twice a year, this does not cause a great deal of difficulty and stocks can be easily maintained, especially with careful warehousing of green coffee beans. Coffee as a commodity, however, is another matter. New technologies, such as the telephone, enabling a transatlantic futures trade, and the railways in Brazil which meant that the crop reached the docks within days of being harvested, changed everything. There were also better storage facilities that protected the coffee bean from all of the ailments that could reduce its quality and its value. It could be warehoused, therefore, until the market moved in the right direction. Better ocean-going transport also brought it to the nations that had a thirst for it more quickly and more efficiently. A supply chain was established in this way and producers had to be part of that or lose out. Sometimes they entered into relationships at the cost of others that had been in existence for generations.

Communications became essential – a ten-minute delay in communicating prices could result in the loss of a great deal of earnings. Of course, as in other areas, modernisation was not all good. It impacted on the way the coffee was produced and when big companies are involved, maximising profit becomes the rallying call, leading, more often than not, to a loss of quality. Standardisation was required by the coffee merchants in other countries, and the old methods could not guarantee that every batch would be of exactly the same quality. The changes in production methods hit small to medium-sized farmers very hard, meaning that they had to find the money to carry out the alterations. In effect, the small farmers lost control of their beans which were sold to large pulping concerns that were owned by foreign companies. Power had shifted to the American and European coffee companies who put up the funding and provided loans for the improvements that had to be made on the plantations.

This was all bad for the nations that produced and relied on their coffee exports. They were more or less victims of the vagaries of the coffee trade in America, Asia and Africa which meant that the price of the product and, therefore, what their farmers might earn, was completely beyond their control. At the turn of the twentieth century, it all came to a head when a series of bumper harvests in Brazil meant that there was an excess of coffee. This was a disaster for coffee farmers as it created falling prices. They were harvesting their crop at a loss.

The Brazilian government's answer was to establish the Coffee Valorisation scheme, a means of supporting coffee prices using a subsidy provided by the government. In this way, farmers could be guaranteed some kind of income. It worked for the farmers but when eventually the warehoused coffee hit the market there was an inevitable glut that brought down prices and worsened the chances of damage to the economy. Ultimately, it was the small farmers who went to the wall. Those supported by global concerns were protected and the wealthier plantation owners either moved on to invest their fortunes elsewhere or weathered the storm.

The Depression did not help the situation as the international price of coffee plummeted. Nonetheless, because of valorisation, with growers continuing to be compensated for their unsold harvests, excess production carried on regardless. In 1932, in an effort to force coffee prices up artificially, the Brazilian National Coffee Council decided to order 18 million sacks of excess coffee to be burned and more than 8 million tons, worth more than $117 million, went up in smoke. Newspapers around the world splashed photographs of the coffee bonfires across their pages, aghast at what the Brazilians were doing. But the crisis did not go away and, for the next ten years, Brazil indulged in this act of national masochism. It became so bad by 1937 that more than 70 per cent of the entire coffee harvest was burnt. Only during the Second World War were efforts made to stabilise the coffee market and ensure that farmers were paid a fair price for their efforts, no matter which country they lived in. In 1940, an agreement was reached – the Inter-American Coffee Agreement. Coffee producers in the Americas would agree to restrictions on their harvests – effectively a quota – on condition that the United States agreed to a restriction on its imports of 15.9 million bags. The Americans were keen to sign the agreement because, with European markets closed because of the war, there was a danger that the decline in the coffee price might drive suffering producer nations into the arms of the Nazis or the Communists. They especially feared for

Brazil. There was an almost immediate effect, and the price almost doubled within a year. It continued to rise until around 1957 when a degree of stability was established.

Producers were eager to maintain the price and this led to the first International Coffee Agreement (ICA), drawn up in 1962 at the United Nations in New York. Signed by producing countries and those that consumed it, its objective was to maintain the quotas of exporting nations and to keep coffee prices not only at a good level but also stable in the market. A year later, under the auspices of the United Nations, given the global economic significance of coffee, the International Coffee Organisation (ICO) was established in London with the objective of overseeing the ICA.

The ICA was not fully implemented until 1965, three years before it was due for re-negotiation. Provision had been made for countries in which it was felt coffee still had to grow in popularity, amongst which were Japan and the Soviet Union. It was decided that the quota system would not be applied to these 'Annex B' nations and countries that were not members of the ICO were also not subject to restrictions. This two-tier price system, however, opened the door to unprincipled dealers who resold these less expensive coffee beans in one of the member states for a greater price. This commodity was given the name 'tourist coffee' because of the tortuous route it took to arrive at its final destination. It presented a serious problem and in 1966, for example, around 20 per cent of the coffee imported into Germany was believed to be 'tourist coffee'.

Coffee surpluses remained a major issue. Eighty-seven

million excess bags of coffee were produced in 1966, almost 75 per cent of which were Brazilian. Africa was also holding a lot of surplus Robusta and science was adding to the problem of over-production. It was discovered that the Cerrado, Brazil's tropical savanna, could support coffee cultivation using zinc and boron which, it had been learned, were essential micronutrients for the coffee plant. With the addition of lime and fertiliser, vast tracts of land could be brought into coffee production. The development of hybrids that produced heavy crops exacerbated the problem. But, in 1968, the Brazilians instituted a plan to destroy huge numbers of older coffee trees, while the ICO's Diversification Fund was used to persuade coffee farmers to start cultivating other crops. Although this was a very practical initiative in Brazil with its huge plantations, it was less practical elsewhere. In Africa, for instance, smallholders were dependent on the few coffee bushes they cultivated and it was not possible for them to diversify.

Meanwhile, the process for adjusting quota levels was difficult and plagued with arguments. Powerful lobbies within the ICO made it difficult for smaller exporting countries. The ICO oversaw the renegotiation of the ICA in 1968, 1976, 1983, 1994 and 2007.

Espresso

The Second World War brought many privations and ersatz coffee became the norm as countries were closed off from imports of the precious bean. Of course, there was no place that suffered more from the absence of a thimbleful of real espresso coffee than Italy. Mussolini was trying, as war approached, to make Italy self-sufficient. Additionally, Italy was facing tariffs and sanctions at the time which put the price of coffee up. So, as early as 1939, Il Duce was keen for Italians to reduce their consumption of coffee. Unsurprisingly, Italians could not countenance being deprived of coffee and Mussolini and his Fascist government knew full well that a coffee shortage would be very bad for morale. He hoped that supplies of beans would increase from North Africa's coffee-growing areas where thousands of Italian colonists, encouraged by him, had gone to settle. The indigenous peoples of the Italian Empire, however, were less than amused and fought a guerrilla war against the occupying Italian forces. This was doubly bad for Mussolini and his intentions, because they destroyed the coffee plantations.

Mussolini next tried to enter into trade deals with the coffee-producing countries, offering arms and military equipment, including planes and submarines, in exchange for coffee beans. It was still not enough and rationing was introduced in April 1939. Coffee supplies had dried up completely by 1941 and Italians had to rely on the black market, with coffee coming in via Switzerland or ersatz coffees being made with ingredients such as barley.

Of course, after the war coffee returned to the coffee machines of Italy and was frothing away around the world where the Italian diaspora had spread itself. There were

Italian people everywhere, from South America, Australia and Africa to Britain and across Europe. American cities such as San Francisco and New York were home to vibrant Italian communities who stayed close to their culture and maintained connections with their family and friends back in the mother country. Everywhere they sent money home to post-war, poverty-stricken Italy and became hubs for Italian goods and services. They opened distinctive cafés and restaurants that championed Italian produce and provided a distribution network for it around the world.

It has to be remembered that, while the Italians were suffering, the Allies were able to enjoy coffee even with the bombs falling or their boys fighting in strange foreign lands. Supplies were still able to get through to Britain and America, for example, from South and Central American coffee-producing countries. All the same, coffee in wartime was often drunk more to keep people alert as they went about their business, or as they actually fought the war, rather than for any inherently pleasant taste sensation. After the war, therefore, the coffee made and served by Italians was like balm, crafted with care and artistry. It was the time of the espresso machine in Australia, Great Britain and Australia and it was embraced by the young people of those countries.

The first espresso machine was patented by Angelo Moriondo (1851-1914) of Turin and displayed at the Turin General Exposition of 1884. An improved version was patented by Luigi Bezzera of Milan in 1901 and this patent was purchased by Desiderio Pavoni in 1905. His company,

La Pavoni, began to produce one a day in his workshop in Milan. The first automatic coffee machine which used steam to extract the flavour from the coffee grounds, arrived in 1933, invented by a Hungarian-Italian, Francesco Illy (1892-1956). He named his company Illycaffè and, branded as Illy, its silver and red cans of coffee are available around the world to this day. The company remains family-owned and employs around 1,200 people. Others entered the espresso machine market, such as Giovanni Achille Gaggia who patented his coffee machine, the first steamless version, in 1938. It used water forced over the coffee grounds at high pressure, producing the crema, the reddish-brown surface layer of froth that is a distinctive characteristic of espresso. Crema is formed when air bubbles combine with fine-ground coffee's soluble oils. Its presence is indicative of a well-ground coffee as well as a skilled barista or coffee maker. It adds a fuller flavour to a cup of espresso as well as a longer after-taste.

The American Coffee Revolution

'He was the guru of everyone in the gourmet coffee revolution. He was the big bang. It all started with him.' That is how Alfred Peet (1920-2007) was described in the *Atlantic* by Corby Kummer, author of the book, *The Joy of Coffee*. Peet's father, Henry, had a coffee-roasting business in Alkmaar in the Netherlands before the Second World War. Aged eighteen, Alfred joined his father's business in 1938, but the war made things very difficult and they were forced to eke out a living by making ersatz coffee from chicory, roasted peas and rye. Alfred ended up in a German labour camp but returned to the family business after the end of the war. By 1948, feeling restless, he travelled to Sumatra and Java, still working in the world of coffee. After a few years in New Zealand, he journeyed to San Francisco, arriving there in 1955. Working for a coffee importer, he was horrified by the poor quality of the beans he was dealing with. It puzzled him that Americans would happily put up with such a low-quality beverage. As he said, 'People drank ten cups of that stuff a day. You knew it had to be weak. If you drank ten cups of strong coffee, you'd be floating on the ceiling'.

Made redundant in 1965, Peet decided to open a shop with a small coffee bar attached. Peet's Coffee & Tea opened in April 1966, on the corner of Vine and Walnut Streets in Berkeley, California. On the day he opened, he had 10 bags of Colombian coffee beans and a 25 pound roaster. The taste of real coffee was strange to some, but any European exiles who dropped in were delighted with what they found. He trained his staff in the arcane art of cupping – smelling, tasting and evaluating different coffees. Peet's was a roaring success and became a favourite spot for the hippies who were then beginning to appear around Berkeley and San Francisco. Famously, every so often, Peet would interrupt the conversation by exclaiming 'I have a roast!' and the coffee purists would rush to the counter.

Around this time, others, tired of the coffee to which Americans had become inured, had the same idea as

Alfred Peet. In New York, Saul Zabar inherited his father's store in the Upper West Side and expanded it, providing his customers with fresh produce. In 1966, he added wholebean coffee to his menu of produce, learning how to cup and roast coffee. He introduced his customers to Kenya AA, Tanzanian peaberry, Hawaiian Kona and other exotic blends, claiming that the roast he produced was lighter than that produced on the West Coast by Alfred Peet. He sold from his store and via a successful mail order business.

By the 1970s, coffee house culture was flourishing not just along both coasts, but also in university towns across the nation and especially in the home of the counter-culture, San Francisco, and in Seattle, Boston and New York. As had been the case centuries before, these new meeting places became hubs for the exchange of new ideas, initiatives and opportunities. An America scarred and humbled by the harrowing years of the Vietnam War, tried to work out its future over cups of Italian espresso. And it was Italian because in the 1970s, the decade when coffee shops were sprouting all over America, Italian-American businesses still controlled the machinery used to brew coffee. The gurgling coffee-dispensing monsters behind the counters were more often than not leased by these companies to café owners who were then bound by service contracts if they wanted the machines to be maintained. Sometimes, even the coffee to be used in them was part of the contract. This could prove very expensive and, if there was a problem with a machine, replacement parts were not always easy to find. Repairs could take some time, especially if your coffee shop was in a town a long way from the big cities. Something had to change.

Starbucks

As the turbulent 1960s faded into history, things did begin to change. People had more disposable income and credit was easy to get and relatively cheap. There was a move by young office workers from the suburbs back into city centres. But as property prices escalated, so did the rent on shops, restaurants, bars and cafés. This squeezed the independent coffee houses that had opened their doors in cities in less expensive times. It meant the end for many and those that survived were forced to focus on the economics of running a business and making a profit rather than becoming the freewheeling community hubs that they had once tried to be. One company provides the link between the hippie ideals of coffee house culture in the 1960s and early 1970s and the global coffee house concerns that would emerge towards the end of the twentieth century – Starbucks.

Starbucks, currently the world's largest coffee house chain and the major player in what is regarded as America's second wave of coffee culture, began in Seattle, Washington, on 30 March, 1971 when Jerry Baldwin (b. 1942), Zev Siegl (b. 1942) and Gordon Bowker (b. 1942) opened their first coffee house near the city's Pike Place Market. Baldwin and Bowker had first bumped into each other at the University of San Francisco, standing in a queue to be allocated dorm places. When it turned out that the dorm was full up, they decided to find an apartment together. They came to know Siegl, who was working for the summer at Seattle's Century 21 World's Fair, after he posted a notice saying that he would be driving to New York, via San Francisco and could take passengers. Bowker, wanting to go to New York before leaving for a trip to Europe, answered his advert and during their time in San Francisco, Siegl was also introduced to Baldwin.

A few years later, the three met up again, after Baldwin had just left the army. He decided to visit Seattle and found himself a job at Boeing, one of the city's biggest employers. Meanwhile, Siegl was teaching history and Bowker was working as a journalist at *Seattle* magazine. The three would regularly meet and come up with schemes to make money. One day, when they were having lunch together, Bowker came up with a life-changing idea. He loved coffee and, in order to find the best quality, he had been driving two and a half hours to Vancouver, British Columbia, in Canada, to a coffee and tea seller called Murchie's. He had spread the word and begun to bring back orders for coffee for friends. There seemed to be a demand for good coffee and he suggested to his two friends that they start a coffee company in Seattle. They leapt on the idea. Anxious to get to grips with the coffee business, Siegl contacted Alfred Peet of Peet's Coffee & Tea in Berkeley and met with him to learn as much as he could about starting and running a coffee shop. Siegl later said of Peet: 'He had a depth of knowledge of coffee that was unparalleled in this country.

There was nobody in his league'. His colleagues Bowker and Baldwin also travelled to Berkeley to have a look at Peet's hugely successful operation and even to work in it to learn as much as they could. Peet agreed to supply them with freshly roasted coffee beans.

Before long, they had located a site for their new venture, on a corner of the old Harbor Heights Hotel at 2000 Western Avenue, Seattle, at a rent of $137.50 a month. Each of the three partners put up $1,500 and they negotiated a $5,000 bank loan. Bowker was by this time running his own advertising agency, working with a designer, Terry Heckler, and as they struggled to find a name for their new business, Heckler suggested that words and names that began with the letters 'ST' were known to be particularly strong and memorable. Then, one day, while staring at an old Californian mining map on the wall of his office, Bowker's eyes fell on a town called Starbo. He immediately connected it with the young chief mate, Starbuck, a character in Herman Melville's classic work of fiction, *Moby Dick*. The company was named Starbucks and Heckler designed a logo featuring a voluptuous bare-breasted mermaid with two tails. The notion was that she was a siren luring customers in to the shop, another maritime allusion to go with the name. The logo has been updated three times since then and its present iteration is a slightly more abstract depiction of a mermaid with no sign of the bare breasts of the original.

To begin with, the store sold coffee beans, tea and spices as well as coffee- and tea-making equipment. They only brewed coffee to showcase what they were selling or to induce people to come into the store to buy something. Initially, Siegl was the business's only paid employee, and the other two partners carried on with their day jobs, although all three could be found working in the store on Saturdays.

They opened a second Starbucks the following year but, as they were still not making much money from the first, they had to borrow from friends to do so. They began roasting their own beans, under Alfred Peet's tuition, and rented a warehouse in which to do their roasting. But, by 1976, the business was struggling. The third store they had opened in Edmonds, north of Seattle, was not doing well and the gourmet cookware they were trying to sell had proved a flop. They closed the Edmonds store and opened instead in Bellevue on the other side of Lake Washington. Then they found out that the building that was home to their first store was due for demolition. They relocated to a location nearby at 1912 Pike Place.

The vagaries of coffee production struck in 1975 when an extraordinary spell of freezing weather devastated the 1975 Brazilian coffee crop. Coffee prices soared and Starbucks was forced to borrow $95,000 just to stay afloat. However, business began to pick up again by 1978. In 1980, Siegl left the company, not relishing the idea of being a corporate manager. By that time, annual sales were up to $4.4 million, a staggering increase of 49 per cent on the previous year. In May 1982, a fifth store was opened on University Way, but this one featured a coffee bar, the first-ever in a

Starbucks. The following September, a New Yorker named Howard Schultz (b. 1953) joined the company as marketing director. He had previously worked as a Xerox salesman and for the Swedish company, Hammerplast, selling drip-brew thermoses. When he walked into Starbucks, he loved it. He would change it beyond recognition.

Schultz was soon pushing for Starbucks to open more outlets selling coffee by the cup and the sixth Seattle store did have a coffee bar. In 1985, they opened in San Francisco and the same year, they purchased Peet's four San Francisco coffee houses and his roasting plant for $3.8 million. A year later, Schultz left Starbucks to launch his own business, Il Giornale Coffee Company, backed to the tune of $150,000 by Starbucks. Bowker left the business in 1987 and Baldwin decided to concentrate on Peet's. Schultz put together some investors and bought Starbucks for $3.8 million.

Rebranding his Il Giornale stores as Starbucks, Schultz embarked on a programme of rapid expansion that first conquered the United States and then the rest of the world. In 1992, with 140 stores across the United States and revenue of $73.5 million, the company went public. By this time, Starbucks stores were roasting more than 2 million pounds of coffee a year and the company was valued at $271 million.

The first Starbucks outside North America was opened in Tokyo in 1996. Two years later, the company launched in the United Kingdom, purchasing and rebranding the 56-outlet Seattle Coffee Company. As the years passed, Starbucks put its sign up around the world, in places such as Australia,

Mexico, South America, Vietnam and Cambodia. It all seemed somehow to come full circle when, in 2016, the company announced its launch in Italy, the twenty-fourth European market it opened. In 2019, it opened its largest-ever store, in Michigan Avenue, Chicago, which has 200 employees. In early 2020, it was operating in over 30,000 locations in more than 70 countries.

In 2000, Schultz had stepped down after 14 years as CEO, moving to the position of global strategist, overseeing Starbucks' international expansion. Then, with the 2008 global financial crisis raging, he returned as CEO. He closed hundreds of branches of the chain, dispensed with the services of countless executives and briefly closed every US Starbucks in order to retrain staff in how to make an espresso. He stepped down once again in 2016, assuming the role of executive chairman. Two years later, he finally retired from active management of Starbucks after 37 years, with several billion dollars in the bank. Amongst the options he was considering was running for the US presidency.

Coffee in the Far East

In the Far East, all the global coffee chains have a presence in the major towns and cities. Of course, visitors to these countries are reassured and made to feel comfortable by these familiar brand names and the locals are happy to feel they are in the mainstream and on a par with those great cities in the West. But the East has its own coffee culture, probably to the surprise of most westerners.

Coffee had colonised the West long before it arrived in the East. In places like Malaysia, with its large Muslim population, it came with merchants from Muslim regions in the West such as Turkey and Arabia. In other places, the colonial powers brought it with them. The French would have taken it to Vietnam in the twentieth century and the Spanish to the Philippines in the eighteenth. It was assimilated wherever it arrived, these countries creating their own relationships with the beverage.

In Singapore, alongside the Western chains, there are home-grown coffee houses serving the traditional local brew – *kopi*. This coffee, made using only Robusta beans, has a distinctive roasting process which involves roasting in palm oil, maize and sugar, which glazes the beans, a variation on the Torrefacto process used in a number of countries such as Spain, France, Portugal, Mexico, Costa Rica, Uruguay and Argentina. These glazed beans are then mixed with normal roasted beans and it is said to provide a strong aroma and taste. Such cafés are very popular, especially as the price of a cup of coffee is far less than what is demanded by the chains.

Barako is the variation of the beverage drunk in the Philippines which was once a major exporter of coffee. Also known as *kapeng barako*, it uses the beans of the coffee varietal, the Liberica which originates in the African state of Liberia. The bean it produces is considered to be harsh in flavour and has an irregular shape. Filipinos took to it, however, naming it *barako* from the Tagalog word for 'manliness'. Coffee first came to the islands in the 1740s with Spanish missionaries and *barako* trees were planted in the lowlands of Lipa in the province of Batangas. It later spread to the neighbouring province of Cavite. In the 1880s, after the coffee rust blight devastated coffee plantations around the world, the Philippines became one of the world's top four coffee exporters. In 1889, however, the country was itself hit by rust, ruining its plantations and forcing farmers to grow other crops instead. Some *barako* trees survived, but when demand for coffee became high once again, the *barako* was sidelined due to the difficulty in cultivating it compared to other varieties. Instead, farmers planted rust-resistant cultivars that were imported from the United States.

Coffee plants were brought to the western Indonesian island of Sumatra by Dutch colonists in 1699. They thrived on the island's rich volcanic soils and Indonesia became the largest coffee-producing nation in the world, 'Java' enjoying a period in history as the world's favourite coffee. The coffee is grown in the Central Highlands and several of the varietals grown, such as Gayo have become world-famous and highly prized. Sumatrans have a unique process known as *Giling Basah* that involves removing the parchment from the bean at around 50 per cent moisture content, in comparison with most other processes where this is done at around 10 to 12 per cent. This gives the green beans a distinctive, dark colour and it is said to be less acidic than coffee from Latin America and Africa. Preparation, too, is different. Water is poured through grounds held in a cloth sieve several times and collected in a large bowl. Somewhat similar to the way Moroccan tea is served, it is then poured from a height into glasses. This aerates the coffee and provides a frothy brew. Starbucks buys a huge amount of Sumatran coffee, using it as a base for its espresso brands.

The Japanese drink more coffee per head than any other Far Eastern country; more, even, than Australians or the British. This is true, even though coffee came to Japan comparatively recently, since the country isolated itself from the West and its cultural influences from 1639 until 1853. The only people who had come into contact with the beverage were the small number who had access to the trading post at Dejima, a small artificial island off the coast of Nagasaki. The island was purpose-built in 1634 to house foreign traders and keep them separate from Japanese, created by digging a canal through the peninsula. The bridge linking it with the mainland was heavily policed. After the end of isolation, however, coffee found the Japanese. One way in which this happened was through Brazil's need for workers on its coffee plantations. Towards the end of the nineteenth century, as we have seen, Italian immigrants were enticed to come to Brazil to work, but their treatment at the hands of the plantation bosses had been so brutal that the Italian government took action to prohibit such subsidised immigration to the country. Another source had to be found and, although the white ruling class of Brazil had restricted the entry of non-Europeans (apart from slaves, of course), they decided in 1908 that Japanese workers would be allowed into the country. A great many took the opportunity to escape poverty back home and many of them would themselves become coffee farmers. This provided a commercial link between Japan and the Brazilian coffee industry and in the twentieth century coffee became popular in Japan. As the century progressed, the affluent Japanese middle class expanded and sought the pleasures that were being enjoyed in the exotic West.

One of the first coffee houses in Japan reflected its connection with the Brazilian coffee industry. Café Paulista opened in Tokyo's fashionable Ginza district in the early years of the new century and was soon a meeting place for writers and artists. Soon the *kissaten* – Japanese for coffee shop – was opening in every town in Japan, frequented mainly by men, and each priding itself on its own unique brew. The coffee was good and some even roasted their own beans. In the cities, women were found in *kissaten* more often, and, as had been the case in the West, specific cafés supported specific interests. By the mid-1930s, there are estimated to have been around 10,000 coffee houses in Tokyo alone.

In the 1960s, Japan began to champion coffee in a can that could be purchased from vending machines. Brewed, blended, and ready to drink, it is available in many varieties, from milky lattes to iced coffee, the labels announcing beans from far-flung places like Hawaii. The fast nature of such a drink matches the fast pace of Japanese city life, busy commuters grabbing a can before being squeezed into a bullet train.

Both Korea and Vietnam experienced war, and the terrible devastation brought about by war, in the twentieth century. Their histories with coffee vary. It was once prohibitively expensive and hard to find in Korea, and Korean cafés, therefore, sold products like *kimchi*, tea and soup. Today, in South Korean cafés, at any rate, it is a staple and affordable to a population that enjoys an affluent lifestyle. In Vietnam, however, there have been extraordinary developments. The French colonised the country in the nineteenth century, bringing with them cuttings from Arabica coffee trees on their Réunion colony in the Indian Ocean. The soil in the Tonkin region, where they were planted, was found to be unsuitable, however. And, with rust disease ravaging plantations around the world, it was decided to plant hardier coffee varietals, the main one being Robusta. With the conflicts the country endured during the twentieth century now a bad memory, coffee is grown in the Annamite Plateau in the Vietnamese Central Highlands.

As would be expected, the country has a huge number of coffee houses or cafés where coffee can be served in the traditional Vietnamese way. It is made at the table. A glass containing condensed milk – used because ordinary milk does not retain its freshness in the searing heat of Vietnam – has a metal filter, a *phin*, placed on it. The filter contains coarse ground coffee and is tamped down. About 60 millilitres of hot water is poured gradually into the *phin*. It is then left for some time – patience is required for Vietnamese coffee – until it has dripped through into the cup. The cup is then stirred to mix the coffee and the condensed milk.

Vietnam is the world's second-largest exporter of coffee after Brazil, and coffee is the country's second-largest agricultural export after rice, with around 1.3 million acres devoted to the cultivation of mostly Robusta beans. It is a business based on smallholdings, with 94 per cent of the coffee produced by half a million tiny family-run farms. Vietnamese coffee represents around 20 per cent of the world's coffee production but the returns are greatly reduced because its green beans are sold directly to large coffee companies to be used in the manufacture of instant coffee. The industry is highly volatile with cycles of boom and bust since the 1980s and smaller farmers bear the brunt of falling prices, making social inequality an important issue in the country.

China

The figures for coffee consumption in China have been historically low. These may have been skewed somewhat by the fact that some of the Chinese population drink no coffee at all, while others consume a great deal. The ethnic mix of the Chinese adds to the confusion, and that is without taking into account the fact that half a million Europeans, Africans and Americans call the country home. Nonetheless, there has traditionally been no coffee culture to speak of in China. There was an element of it once, in the nineteenth century, when, as a result of defeat in the Opium Wars, China was forced to cede large chunks of its territory to the Western powers. Britain, the USA, Belgium, France, Russia, Austria, Germany, Italy and the Netherlands all occupied concessions from which they could trade and, basically, suck China dry. Of course, they brought their culture with them and part of that culture was drinking coffee. Coffee houses thrived in locations such as the Bund in Shanghai, the wealthy centre of foreign occupation from the 1860s to the 1930s. Meanwhile, in a special part of the International Settlement area in Shanghai in the 1930s, there was an area for stateless refugees, home to 20,000 Jews fleeing persecution in Europe. Seedy cafés sold coffee in this area where there was the rare sight of Europeans and Chinese mixing socially.

The French established coffee plantations in the southern province of Yunnan towards the end of the nineteenth century. Given the soil and weather conditions, they planted Arabica. Most Chinese, however, drink Robusta these days, in the form of instant coffee and made mostly from beans imported from Vietnam.

The largest coffee-growing area in Yunnan is Pu'er, located in the south of the province. Pu'er was famous for a long time as a high quality tea-growing area, but now has around 100,000 acres given over to coffee which is mostly purchased by the global chains. Coffee production on a large scale began in Yunnan in 1988 when the Chinese government went into partnership with the World Bank and the United Nations Development Program to promote coffee cultivation there. Around that time, Nestlé also became involved in coffee production in the province. The results of all this activity were staggering. The ICO tells us that between 1994 and 2004, coffee production rose by 21 per cent and by the same amount between 2004 and 2014. By that time, China was producing 114,000 metric tons, making it the 13th-largest coffee producing nation in the world, just above Costa Rica, and it will undoubtedly continue to grow. The beans are bought by large businesses such as Nestlé, to be made into instant coffee but other large names like global merchant firm, the Louis-Dreyfus Company, the trading house Volcafé, and Starbucks have also been purchasing them recently. Chinese coffee beans are also being sold into the domestic market in increasing amounts, either for instant coffee or to be used for commercial roasted coffee. Some producers are even beginning to move into higher quality speciality coffees. Better practices on the farms and wet/dry mill processing are producing better quality.

Even without a coffee culture, coffee drinking in China, home of tea, has become fashionable, adopted by young, white collar city-dwellers, government officials and teachers who are eager to replicate the lifestyle of affluent Westerners. Branches of European and American coffee houses abound. After entering the market in 1999, Starbucks now has 60 per cent of it, with more than 4,300 outlets in 180 Chinese cities. Nonetheless, many other Western companies have a presence there, including Britain's Costa Coffee, Canada's Tim Horton's, America's Dunkin' Donuts and the Swiss company Nestlé.

Coffee's Third Wave

The three ages of coffee could be said to have begun with the 'first wave', that some suggest began in the nineteenth century when brands like Folgers started to appear in every household. People began to drink increasing amounts of coffee and, by the 1960s, it was affordable and accessible to all. The first wave was all about pre-ground, vacuum-packed, mass market cans of coffee from major brands such as Maxwell House and the aforementioned Folgers. This coffee was purchased from a grocer for consumption at home and there was no concern about the coffee's origin or even what type it was. The objective was for every pack to contain the same quality coffee and to produce a beverage uniform in aroma and flavour. It was low-priced to the extent that many restaurants were happy to offer free refills.

The 'second wave' is widely acknowledged to have been started, as we have seen, by Peet's Coffee and Tea in Berkeley, California, which brought a more artisanal approach to the sourcing, roasting and blending of its coffee beans. Countries of origin were flagged and their coffee had a signature dark roast profile. Peet's proved inspirational to the founders of Starbucks who launched their chain in Seattle. The generic cup of coffee now gave way to coffees from different countries with different flavour characteristics. The second wave also introduced to the market coffee-based beverages, in particular those made with espresso that were indigenous to Italy. Coffee was now purchased in a location that emphasised lifestyle and the local, individually owned coffee shops were edged out of business by large chains that were run as profitable businesses.

Inspired originally by the three waves of feminism, the term 'third wave' originated in an article in the Roasters' Guild newsletter, 'Norway and Coffee', written by Trish Rothgeb, a San Francisco café-owner, then living in Oslo, and the first woman to become qualified as one of the Q-Graders, the master evaluators of the quality of coffee. The Q was established by the Coffee Quality Institute a couple of decades ago. Taking about three years to pass, it qualifies the holder to accurately evaluate the taste and locate any defects in any coffee, allowing only a tiny margin of error that is calibrated against every other Q-Grader in the world. Q-Graders use a 100 point scale and if a coffee achieves 80 or more, it is designated 'specialty'. This means it has a high-quality taste and is low on defects. Defects that could be detected are such things as insect holes, small stones and chipped coffee bean husks. It is an expensive process and only coffees that are most likely going to score the required points are entered, which means that most are not.

Now, everyone talks about a 'third wave', led by consumers and manufacturers, in which the old, traditional ways of growing coffee and making it are being re-evaluated. The coffee revolution has moved on from where you drink it to what is actually in the cup. In the third wave, every element of the supply chain becomes important to the quality of the coffee experience – the producer/grower, the importer, the roaster, the barista and the consumer. The aims are, above all, to increase the quality of the coffee we are being offered; to ensure that it is obtained more often by direct trade; that lighter roast profiles are pursued; and that innovative brewing methods are explored.

So, third wave coffee is really about three things – artisanship, aesthetic and traceability. Third wavers treat coffee almost in the same way that oenophiles treat wine. Tasting coffee in the way that many other commodities from whisky to cheese are tasted in order to define their qualities is becoming popular. Each different coffee in this category tells its own story, the struggles of the farmer, the intricacies of the agricultural process, the individual characteristics of the product – each of these has a tale to tell, and third-wavers are eager to listen.

The aesthetics of the coffee-drinking experience itself are important in the third wave, especially the visual aesthetic. Design has an influence on the experience and even something as basic as the shape of the coffee mug will leave its mark on the coffee-drinking experience. The décor and architecture of the coffee house are also very important to the third waver. Large, hissing coffee machines are anathema in this world. Rather individual cups of coffee are brewed, slow-dripped into the cup to preserve the flavour and aroma. And coffee-consumption in this arena is a multi-sensory experience. Even better is the knowledge and technique of the third wave baristas. They know their coffee and are passionate about it in the same way as the employees of a really good wine shop will sing the praises of a particular wine – although, of course, in a wine shop you are not called on to make a glass of wine on the spot. The good barista will have cupping notes for the coffees on offer and will know the correct brew methods to employ, perhaps using one of the many new coffee brewing devices.

Traceability is key to coffee's third wave and here social responsibility plays a big part, people wanting reassurance that, in an industry with a history of exploitation, human dignity is part of the value chain. Thus many aficionados now want to know exactly where all the money goes that they pay for their coffee.

Single-origin coffee is important in this new coffee movement. To know that it is the work of one farmer or producer and thus to know the country, the region and even the elevation at which the coffee bushes are grown is the Holy Grail. Each individual coffee will showcase the characteristics and complex flavours that are unique to its place of origin. Roasting, too, is considered and nowadays a light roast will be favoured over a dark roast, since the light roast does not kill the flavours, but allows them to make their presence felt in the coffee.

Climate Change and the Coffee Industry

The climate impact of the single-use coffee cup has, of course, been recognised for some time and much is already being done by governments, coffee chains and consumers to remedy this problem. Other issues such as a reduction in carbon emissions in the supply chain, the conservation of water used in both direct operations and coffee production and a decrease in the amount of waste sent to landfill are also high on the agenda of the major players in the industry. But, as the International Coffee Organisation has acknowledged, climate change is likely to have a far more profound impact on coffee consumption in the coming decades. Indeed, the ICO forecasts that rising temperatures may well render some current coffee-producing areas no longer viable, jeopardising not just our regular coffee fix, but also endangering the livelihoods of millions of small coffee-growers.

Columbia University's Center on Sustainable Investment has projected that as much as 75% of the land that is currently used in the production of Arabica coffee beans - as we have seen, the variety that is most commonly used by roasters – will be decimated by climate change by 2050 if nothing is done. We know that lower temperatures ensure the slower ripening of coffee beans which is conducive to the development of the necessary complex acids and sugars. Increases in temperature will, therefore, have an adverse impact on flavour and quality and, eventually, when it becomes too hot, the coffee plant will simply be unable to survive. Indeed, farmers are already feeling the effects of climate change with rises in temperature, droughts, weather events and the increased incidence of pests and diseases such as rust. A failure to take the necessary steps will almost certainly lead to increased prices for consumers, a decline in quality and even shortages. The prospect of a dwindling supply of its product is, of course, a huge problem for the coffee industry, especially as population growth and an increasing thirst for its product in Asia, Africa and elsewhere is likely to double global demand for coffee by 2050.

In a report by The Climate Institute, it is recommended that coffee consumers play their part in dealing with this serious issue by drinking only carbon neutral coffee. Those working in the coffee supply chain are, at the same time, being urged to engage with coffee farming communities to help them adapt to climate change and to reduce carbon emissions. At a Starbucks-owned 600-acre coffee farm in the Costa Rican province of Alajuela, as well as in other locations, World Coffee Research, a non-profit organisation that has the backing of some of the world's biggest coffee players, is developing new varieties of coffee beans that are being tested for productivity, resistance to disease and, of course, flavour. The aim is to find a bean that can stand up to the threats of drought and heat, but can also achieve the required quality standards.

However, as one of the authors of the Columbia Center report has warned, it is not possible to simply breed our way out of the impact of climate change. Governments and the coffee industry must work in tandem to help farmers survive, to provide them with up-to-date information on pests and, with water resources increasingly coming under pressure, to introduce the necessary irrigation. Farmers may even need help to re-locate their farms to cooler areas and Starbucks is already providing loans to farmers for infrastructure projects. If such help is not provided, the twenty million or so coffee-growers around the world will have no other option than to uproot their coffee plants and plant other crops. Their vast stores of knowledge and experience will be lost forever.

Without a concerted effort to combat climate change, coffee will almost certainly still be around in 2050, but it might be a good deal more expensive and it might not taste as good.

Appendix

A Short History of Coffee-Making Equipment

In the West, when coffee first arrived, it was made in the way that Turks make it to this day. Finely ground coffee is mixed in water and sugar and heated in a *cezve* – a small copper pot with a long handle – before being poured into a cup or dish. The grounds settle in the bottom of the cup leaving the rest of the coffee clear and flavoursome.

Soon, however, people began to try to make improvements to the coffee-making process. For a long time, the French led the way. The first version that moved away from the Turkish method involved placing the ground coffee in a linen bag and then infusing it with hot water. This avoided having the dregs settle on the bottom of the cup and eliminated the possibility of accidentally drinking them. It was also discovered at some point that coffee should not be made using boiling water. If the water is too hot, the coffee's delicate, fragile, volatile essences are destroyed and they are what lend the drink much of its flavour. To ensure a good cup of coffee, the water should be at a temperature that is just below boiling point.

The first radical departure from the Turkish method came at the start of the nineteenth century when the extremely long-lived Archbishop of Paris, Jean Baptiste Comte de Belloy (1709-1808), invented the first drip coffee pot, giving inspiration to many inventors in England, France and the United States. There were three elements to his device. The ground coffee was placed in the upper container which was stacked on top of an empty lower container that was positioned on top of a pot. In between the two was placed a cloth filter. Hot water was then poured over the grounds, allowing the coffee to slowly drip through the cloth, and any solids were filtered out. The liquid collected in the pot below. However, the prospective drinker had to exercise considerable patience as the process took some time. As a result, when he finally raised the cup to his lips, his coffee might be only lukewarm. De Belloy's innovation was never patented. The first French patent for a coffee-maker was granted to Denobe, Henrion and Rouch in 1802, for a 'pharmacological-chemical coffee-making device by infusion'. In that same year, the Englishman Charles Wyatt (1758-1819) was granted a patent for an apparatus for distilling coffee.

Sir Benjamin Thompson (1753-1814) was an American-born British scientist and inventor who had fought on the Loyalist side in the American Revolutionary War. Moving to London after the war, he was knighted and appointed a full colonel. He later became Army Minister in the Bavarian government and, in 1791, was made a count of the Holy Roman Empire as Count Rumford. This extraordinary man was also a prolific inventor, designing improvements for fireplaces, chimneys, kitchen ranges, boilers and industrial furnaces. He also invented a means of keeping coffee warm as it dripped into a pot. On a trip to France, he enhanced Archbishop Belloy's drip coffee pot by encasing it in an insulating jacket that could be filled with hot water, thereby helping the coffee pot to stay warm during the long dripping process.

A drip-brew coffee maker with three chambers that was heated on a stove is said to have been invented by a Parisian tinsmith named Morize in 1819. Called the 'Napoletana', it derives its name from the fact that, at the time, Naples was one of the largest coffee-importing ports. This device, made of copper until 1886 when the material changed to aluminium, consists of a bottom section filled with water, a middle filtering section filled with ground coffee, and an upside-down pot placed on top. When the water boils on the stove, the entire three-part coffeemaker is turned upside down so that the hot water can pass through the grounds and through the filter. Once this has happened, the two sections for boiling the water and filtering are removed, leaving the coffee to be served from the remaining pot. It was similar to an invention patented by a Frenchman named Hadrot in 1806.

Also in 1819, the first patent for a pumping coffee percolator was granted to the Frenchman Joseph-Henry-

Marie Laurens. It involved the rising of boiling water, heated on a stove, through a tube, forming a continuous cycle. His design was improved upon in 1827 by another Frenchman, Jacques-Augustin Gandais. His device consisted of two chambers, the top connected to the bottom by a tube. Water would be taken up the tube when boiling, into the top chamber where it was sprayed over the ground coffee, the liquid then dripping down into the now-empty bottom chamber.

The glass vacuum coffee pot was the next step, helped by improvements in glass manufacture and its greater availability. A better understanding of fluid mechanics and vacuums also paved the way for this innovation. The first patent in this area was granted to a Frenchwoman, Jeanne Richard, in 1838. She based her idea on an existing pot made by a German company, Loef. What was described as the 'French Balloon' design was perfected three years later by another Frenchwoman, a Madame Vassieux of Lyons. The French Balloon was a design so attractive that, instead of being kept out of sight in a kitchen cupboard, it was proudly displayed in the dining room so that drinkers could be delighted by its workings. It was made up of two globes, one sitting on top of the other, connected by a tube that stretched to the bottom of the lower globe. At the top opening of the tube was a filter. The water was poured into the bottom globe while into the upper one went the ground coffee. The water was heated by a candle or lamp and, as it expanded in the heat, it was forced up the tube to mix with the coffee powder in the upper globe. When most of the water had been evacuated from the lower globe, and the mixing of water and coffee had been going on for a time suitable to the type of coffee desired, the heat source was extinguished and a partial vacuum occurred, drawing the coffee through the filter and into the bottom globe, ready to be served.

A further enhancement to this type of coffee-maker was made by a Scottish inventor, James Napier (1821-79) in 1850, with two glass containers being placed side by side and connected by a siphon tube. The glass vacuum pot was revived in America in 1915 by two sisters from Massachusetts, Anne Bridges and Mrs Sutton. They used the newly invented Pyrex glass which was strong and heat-resistant to create their Silex coffee pot. It became so successful in the USA that it was used as the generic name for any glass vacuum pot.

In 1850, there was another development in coffee-making equipment when a pot with a fine mesh screen attached to a plunger was introduced. The mesh was made possible by the Industrial Revolution and the device was improved on by two Frenchmen named Mayer and Delforge. Their 'infusion coffee maker', patented in 1852, was not perfect as the mesh failed to hug the sides completely and the ground coffee could leak through. This flaw was eliminated in the 1930s by Italians Attilio Calimani and Giulio Moneta who added a spring coiling around the filter's edge. The final amendment, and the one used in the modern-day press-pot, was to extend the mesh screen beyond the coiled spring and turn it up at the edge. This *cafetière à piston filtrant*, as it was called, was the invention of a Swiss man, Fallero Bondanini, in 1959.

Many were interested in the use of steam pressure to make coffee. If water could be put under a pressure higher than 1 atmosphere (our normal pressure on Earth), could it possibly produce a more flavoursome coffee? An Italian, Luigi Bezzera, built a machine that forced steam and boiling water through coffee grounds at 1.5 atmospheres and it took only a matter of seconds. Thus 'espresso', meaning 'fast', got its name. Bezzera sold his patent in 1903 to Desidero Pavoni and he marketed the espresso machine across the world.

The coffee that resulted, although richer and more complex than previously, was often bitter because the water and steam were too hot. The machines were difficult to operate and the pressure was insufficient to create the rich *crema* on top of the drink that today signifies a coffee of high quality. Nonetheless, espresso took off, especially in Italy where the local espresso bar became a second home to countless men.

In 1933, in order to provide that espresso experience at home, the Italian inventor, Alfonso Bialetti (1888-1970) created a variation on the original pumping percolator – the famous Moka Pot. Made of aluminium, it comes in three sections. In the bottom container is the water. A filter basket, with a tube coming out of the bottom, holds the coffee powder. Screwed onto these two is the empty upper container which has a rubber gasket on the bottom to ensure a tight seal, and a second metal filter. The pot is heated on a stove until a gurgling noise tells the drinker that the hot water, under pressure, is being forced upwards, through the grounds and into the upper chamber. It is then served. Improvements in manufacturing and a safety release valve ensured that similar pressures could be achieved to that in the La Pavoni machine, but at home. Sadly, those men who had lived at the espresso bar no longer had a valid excuse for going there. Good espresso could be made at home. Needless to say, the Moka Pot became immensely successful.

Meanwhile, in the coffee bars there were also changes. As we have seen, in 1947, Giovanni Achille Gaggia patented his new style of espresso machine with its lever releasing hot water and then when it was released forcing the water through the coffee at very high pressure. The result was a superior coffee with that much desired froth on top, the *crema*.

Finally, in 1960, Ernesto Valente, of the Milan company Fabbrica Apparecchiature Elettromeccaniche e Affini (FAEMA), designed a machine that used an electric pump to pressurise the water and pass it through the coffee grounds. It was capable of creating nine atmospheres of pressure – the pressure that is used to make modern espresso.

Bibliography

Ellis, Markman, *The Coffee House: A Cultural History*, London: Weidenfeld & Nicolson, 2011

Hoffmann, James, *The World Atlas of Coffee: From Beans to Brewing*, London: Mitchell Beazley, 2018

Morris, Jonathan, *Coffee: A Global History*, London: Reaktion Books, 2018

Pendergrast, Mark, *Uncommon Grounds: The History of Coffee and How it Transformed the World*, New York: Basic Books, 2010

Ukers, William H, *All About Coffee*, New York: The Tea and Coffee Trade Journal Company, 1922

Wild, Antony, *Black Gold: The Dark History of Coffee*, New York: Harper Perennial, 2010

Index

●LDCASTLE BOOKS

POSSIBLY THE UK'S SMALLEST
INDEPENDENT PUBLISHING GROUP

Oldcastle Books is an independent publishing company formed in 1985 dedicated to providing an eclectic range of titles with a nod to the popular culture of the day.

Imprints vary from the award winning crime fiction list, NO EXIT PRESS, to lists about the film industry, KAMERA BOOKS & CREATIVE ESSENTIALS. We have dabbled in the classics, with PULP! THE CLASSICS, taken a punt on gambling books with HIGH STAKES, provided in-depth overviews with POCKET ESSENTIALS and covered a wide range in the eponymous OLDCASTLE BOOKS list. Most recently we have welcomed two new digital first sister imprints with THE CRIME & MYSTERY CLUB and VERVE, home to great, original, page-turning fiction.

oldcastlebooks.com

OLDCASTLE BOOKS		KAMERA BOOKS		HIGHSTAKES PUBLISHING
POCKET ESSENTIALS		CREATIVE ESSENTIALS		THE CRIME & MYSTERY CLU
NO EXIT PRESS		PULP! THE CLASSICS		VERVE BOOKS